ARE YOU *SURE* YOU WANT TO BE A LANDLORD?

A PRACTICAL GUIDEBOOK WITH ADVICE, HUMOR, STORIES AND PHOTOS FROM A REAL LANDLORD

THESE STORIES ARE NOT FROM A MOVIE OR COMEDY SHOW THEY ARE REAL LIFE STORIES

Cathy Keeton Azar

Copyright © 2013

Published by Warren Publishing, Inc.
Huntersville, NC
www.warrenpublishing.net

Library of Congress Control Number: 2013914163

ISBN: 978-0-9894814-2-7

This publication contains the ideas and opinions of the author. It is intended to provide informative material on the subject addressed in the publication. The author makes no claims or representation to be rendering professional services. If the reader requires professional advice or consultation, they should consult the appropriate professional. The author and publisher specifically disclaim all responsibility, loss or risk incurred as a consequence of the use and application of any of the content of this book and neither shall be held liable for damages arising from the contents of this book. The author and publisher make no representations or warranties with respect to the accuracy or completeness of the contents of this book. The advice and strategies contained in this book may not be suitable for every situation.

Any organization or website referred to in this book as a source of further information does not mean that the author or publisher endorse the information or organization or any information/recommendations on that website. The websites may have changed or are no longer in existence between this book was written and when it is read.

Landlord/tenant laws and ordinances vary from state to state. The author provided information from the state that they reside in. The reader should check the landlord/tenant laws and ordinances for their own particular state. If in doubt, the reader should consult the advice of an attorney or other professional source.

ACKNOWLEDGMENTS

Thanks to my real estate partner husband. When we invested in real estate years ago, we had no idea that we would become landlords. As professionals, we had to learn all kinds of new skills. It has been a learning experience that has required lots of patience and diplomacy. My husband is in a lot of these stories and had the patience to deal with them.

Thanks to our son who after learning the positive and negatives about being a landlord and still wants to do it. Thank goodness, we are able to laugh about all the experiences of being a landlord.

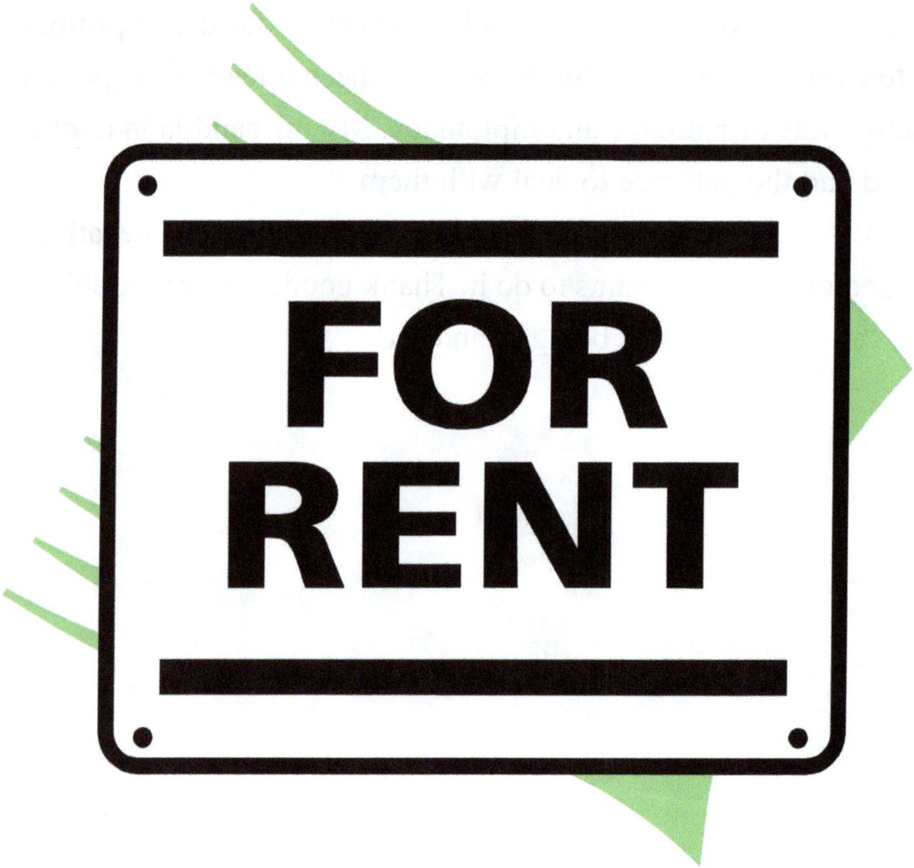
FOR
RENT

TABLE OF CONTENTS

SOCIAL SECURITY REFERENCE NUMBERS

WEBSITE RESOURCES FOR LANDLORDS

INTRODUCTION:
WHAT IS A LANDLORD?

DEFINITION:
An owner of a property that rents or leases that property under an agreement.

Their obligation is to perform all the covenants into which they entered in making the lease agreement. They have to secure that the tenant has quiet enjoyment of the premises leased and the landlord is bound by the agreement to repair the premises as stated in the agreement and not to perform wrongful eviction. The landlord's rights are to receive the rent as agreed upon and to be able to enforce all the terms of the lease agreement. The tenant must treat the premises such that no damages are done to the property. The landlord has the right to have possession of their property upon the expiration of the lease.

These days more and more people are investing in rental property. It is a "buyer's market," where properties can be purchased through foreclosures, short sales and auctions. All real estate in every city, town and neighborhood that is rented out is owned by a landlord. People are buying properties for rental purposes. It seems like a smart investment — but can everyone be a landlord? Owning a property and being the landlord of a property are two different things. What skills does it take to be a landlord? Do you have enough capital to invest in real estate and to make a profit? Are you a hands-on type of person? Can you fix things? Are you diplomatic with people? Are you easily shocked? These are all questions that potential landlords should ask themselves before diving into the rental property business. If you don't have a manager to handle your properties, you will be the one doing it all. You will have to be a jack-of-all-trades and wear many different hats. You will have to have skills in advertising, selling, screening, negotiating, construction, repairs, maintenance, property management, collection and lease enforcement.

This book will provide you with basic guidelines on what to do as a landlord. It will also guide you with recommendations on how to prevent problems with your tenants. It is told by a landlord with over twenty years' experience. These are first hand experiences told from a landlord's perspective. Some of the experiences are pretty strange and their accompanying photos are strange as well. But it is all true and could happen to any landlord. You can learn how to be prepared for the worst case scenario. You may be thinking that a landlord just sits back and collects money each month but that is far from the truth. The landlord works hard for his money. It is not a 9-5 job — it is a 24-7 job. The landlord gets calls in the middle of the night and while on vacation. The landlord sees things from people that most people will never see in their lifetime. Remember that some tenants do not take care about the landlord's property because it is not their own. They do things to the property that you would never expect. The stories in this book appear humorous but at the time they occurred, they were far from humorous for the landlord. The stories are about "tenants from hell." They are the kind of tenants that the landlord never thought he would come across in his business. The stories are all true and the photos are actual photos taken by the author/landlord. The book is divided into chapters that have lessons. There are twenty-five lessons that should be followed. If the landlord doesn't follow these lessons, they can expect some problems. This book will illustrate what some of those problems are and how to avoid them. There isn't any way that a landlord would know about these kinds of encounters and situations unless they were advised of them. There isn't any legal guide that would prepare you for what this book will describe.

This book is not a legal guide and shouldn't be used for that purpose. If you need legal advice for your rental properties, you should seek it. The purpose of this book is to provide prospective landlords with tips and recommendations that will save them time, trouble and money, all told from a humorous point of view. The author and her husband have been investing in real estate for over twenty years. They have purchased properties specifically for rental purposes. They have rented residential single family dwellings, apartments, condos and commercial properties. They have learned along the way, sometimes making the right decisions and sometimes the wrong ones. Every rental property has provided a learning experience. It takes years of experience to learn what they as landlords have learned. Once you learn from your mistakes, hopefully you won't make them again. From making the lease to filing eviction papers, these landlords have done it all. They have come across some pretty horrific situations. That is why they wanted to write this book. They are sharing their real life experiences to help existing landlords and/or those wanting to become a landlord. This is the type of book that provides the basic guidelines for what you need to do to become a landlord. These real life experiences will provide more insight into being a landlord. Once the reader reads this book, they can make an informed decision as to whether or not they are capable of being a landlord (or whether they need to invest in hiring a management team). You can profit from owning rental properties. You can even become wealthy. To gain wealth in this business, you have to be knowledgeable and have some experience. It also takes lots of work and the willingness to learn the needed skills. Hopefully, the reader will never encounter some of the problems in this book but anything can happen! Humor goes a long way in life. Good luck, you will need it!

CHARACTERISTICS OF A GOOD LANDLORD

1. The landlord knows how to purchase their properties.

2. The landlord knows how to screen tenants.

3. The landlord has business skills.

4. The landlord is diplomatic with people.

5. The landlord knows how to do minor repairs and fix things.

6. The landlord learns the landlord/tenant laws for their state.

7. The landlord has patience.

8. The landlord keeps working capital.

9. The landlord is firm but fair.

10. The landlord maintains their properties.

CHAPTER 1:
KNOW HOW TO PURCHASE YOUR PROPERTY

Any person who is thinking about investing in real estate for the purpose of rental income has a lot to consider, beginning with which property to buy. Purchasing the wrong property will be a disaster for the prospective landlord. It is the most important decision that you as a landlord will make. After all, you are planning on making income from the property. If you don't make income, what is the point in purchasing real estate? There are certain criteria that you should look at before you purchase the property. First of all, do you want to rent residential property or commercial property? There is a big difference in these two types of rental property. Most people begin their career in real estate investment with residential. The average person will be more familiar with residential than renting a commercial property. The following is a list of things that should be examined carefully before jumping into a real estate investment career.

1. **FIND A QUALIFIED REAL ESTATE BROKER TO HELP YOU FIND THE TYPE OF PROPERTY YOU ARE LOOKING FOR.** However, if you are experienced with real estate, you may be able to find your own property. A real estate broker will be able to assist you in finding bank foreclosures and short sales. Sometimes these types of bank sales offer the prospective buyer a much better deal. The price will be lower if you are willing to do repairs to the property. If you are new to real estate investing, consult a real estate broker.

2. **KNOW WHICH TYPE OF RENTAL PROPERTY YOU WANT TO INVEST IN.** Do you want residential or commercial? Be aware that each type of rental requires different skills on your part. Commercial property will probably be more expensive to purchase but it will also bring a higher income. Know the market. Is the market strong or is it slow in the area where you live? Do you want property only in the area where you reside or are you willing to purchase property in another town? Study the market to know comparable properties and the high and low prices of those properties. Are foreclosures strong in the area where you want to purchase property? Can you truly afford to purchase the properties you are considering?

3. **'LOCATION, LOCATION, LOCATION,' CANNOT BE SAID ENOUGH.** The location is the key rule for real estate. Do you want property in the city or in a country-type setting? Is the property accessible to you? Do you want to travel to the property when it needs repairs? How far are you willing to travel? Is the area safe or is it a high crime area? You can call the local police department to check on the crime statistics for the area. If the crime rate is high, you may want to reconsider whether you should invest in that area. Do the properties in the area hold their value? Is the property depreciation high or low for the area? Does the property have septic or sewer? If it has sewer, you need to know that there may be more repairs due to sewer problems. Does the property have well water or city water? With well water, there may be more repairs, as well. These are some of the factors that must be examined before you purchase.

4. **INSPECT THE PROPERTY BEFORE YOU PURCHASE.** If you are handy when it comes to repairs and know a lot of home maintenance you may be able to do a thorough inspection yourself, however, most people need a professional to do an inspection. The roof, the plumbing, the electrical, the heating and the cooling are all major items that need inspection. Is there any structural damage or evidence of flooding or water damage? Check for mold, radon, lead paint and any other potentially hazardous item. Don't overlook anything because you will be stuck with big repair bills.

5. **COMPARE THE GOING RATES OF RENTS FOR THE PROPERTIES IN THE AREA.** Is the property you are considering purchasing going to fall within those price ranges? What is the average mortgage payment or rent? If the properties are only renting for $500 per month, it may not allow you to make any money. Know if the property is in a high-priced, middle-priced or low-priced area.

6. **MAKE SURE THAT YOU ARE PURCHASING PROPERTY THAT WILL ALLOW YOU TO MAKE A PROFIT.** If you can't make a profit, why purchase the property? Do you want a headache for nothing? Do not invest in something that is priced too high. It is one thing to pay cash for a property and another to have a mortgage payment. If you are going to have a mortgage payment, you need to get a return on your money within 5 years. If you purchase a property for say, $100,000, you need $20,000 per year in rental income to return that money in 5 years. Calculate these figures carefully. The monthly rent payment should be at least 50% more

than your mortgage payment. If your mortgage payment is $500 per month, rent needs to be at least $750-$1,000 per month. Remember, you won't pocket the difference because you will have expenses. You still have to calculate property taxes, insurance, repair and maintenance expenses. One of the biggest mistakes that landlords make is to overpay for the property and they never manage to recoup their investment. Don't let your rent be eaten up by expenses that you didn't calculate. Figure out all of your expenses before you purchase a property.

7. **WHO WILL YOUR TENANTS BE?** When choosing a property be aware of the income bracket that you are choosing. If the property is in a high income area, your tenants will have higher incomes, as well. If it is in a low income area, expect low income tenants. Are you comfortable with tenants in all income brackets?

8. **ALL PROPERTIES REQUIRE MAINTENANCE.** Are you capable of doing any or all of the maintenance yourself? Will you have to hire people to do all repairs and maintenance? This is a cost that you must figure into the rent. You will always have to do maintenance - both large and small. Regular maintenance includes the heating/ ac system, plumbing, roof, painting, flooring etc. It is very helpful to your income if you can do at least some of the maintenance yourself.

9. **EXPENSES MUST BE CALCULATED.** Figure what expenses must be covered by the rent each month. Deduct from the rent all expenses including the maintenance, repairs, property taxes and

insurance and see whether you can cover everything and still profit. The taxes and insurance are fixed expenses. Hopefully, the maintenance and repair expenses only occur occasionally but you still have to calculate them from your monthly rents.

10. **LEASES AND RECORD KEEPING ARE A PART OF THE DEAL.** The landlord must have a solid lease for all the tenants that protects his interests. If you aren't comfortable making the lease, consult an attorney to draw one up. The lease may be yearly, monthly or even weekly. The lease must include many things and it needs to be examined carefully to make sure all the landlord's bases are covered. You must also keep accurate records for tax purposes. If you want to claim a deduction for all your repairs, you will need to have records and receipts. You will also need accurate records in order to evict a tenant and in case you have to go to court.

11. **IF YOU PURCHASE A COMMERCIAL PROPERTY, THERE ARE GOING TO BE STATE, LOCAL AND COUNTY ORDINANCES AND RULES YOU WILL HAVE TO FOLLOW.** The commercial property will be rented to a business that must follow these ordinances, as well. That tenant will also have to get permits. As the landlord, you may or may not have to outfit the property to suit the tenant. There will be a different set of guidelines for the landlord that includes more expenses. However, the landlord can probably expect to collect a higher rent on a commercial property than on a residential property. For example if you rent to a retail tenant, there may be the need to have handicapped accessible bathrooms, parking signs, designated parking spaces and other

specific rules that have to be complied with. After the tenant's lease expires, you may rent to a different type of business and have to comply with a different set of rules. In other words, you may get higher rent but you will also have higher expenses.

As you can see, being a landlord requires some knowledge and expertise. You can't just go out and buy a property and collect the rent. You need to make a wise property purchase, do your homework on the property, calculate all your costs, figure your profit, become familiar with leases, keep thorough records, and somehow take care of maintenance and repairs. Experience will guide you along if you can follow the steps given here on how to make a wise purchase and how to make a profit.

PURCHASE TO PROFIT

CHAPTER 2:
THE LANDLORD MUST MEET THE PROSPECTIVE TENANT IN PERSON

The landlord should never rent to tenants over the telephone, over the internet or through friends or relatives. The landlord must meet the tenant in person or else there will be real potential for problems. Things aren't always as they seem over the telephone or internet. The following true story proves this point. It is a situation where the landlord made the decision to rent their property over the internet. The landlord thought that since the prospective tenant's father lived locally, it would be acceptable for the father to inspect the property for his son. The entire transaction was done over the internet. Wrong decision! The following story shows why this is a bad idea.

THE OUT OF TOWN TENANTS

The landlord had just placed his property for rent. The former tenant had left unexpectedly and left the place in a mess. They had moved in the night without giving notice even though they had a 6 month lease. The landlord found the place left with old bedroom furniture and an old sofa the tenants purposely didn't take due to their poor condition. The floors were un-swept and the carpet was filthy and stained. Food had been left in the refrigerator. The worst part was that the tenants had also left roaches. The landlord had never seen roaches in all his years of renting. But he even found them in the kitchen cabinets when he inspected the house. It took around a month to clean and repair the house. Once it was done, the landlord placed an ad for the property on Craigslist. The ad was very specific and listed all the leasing requirements as well as photos of the house. Everything was in order once again. There were several responses, some people provided phone numbers and others didn't. The landlord assumed that the people who provided phone numbers would be more serious so he called them first. After going through a list of prospects, he called a person with an odd phone number that turned out to be a California number. The person was living in California and hoping to return back to his native North Carolina.

"I am originally from Charlotte, North Carolina but have been living in California for the past 5 years. I have a wife and one child," the man explained to the landlord.

"Do you have employment lined up when you get to North Carolina?" the landlord asked.

"My dad lives in Charlotte and has a job lined up for me. They are just waiting for me to relocate," he explained.

"Do you know the area that my property is located in?" asked the landlord, trying to do some screening of the tenant over the phone.

"Yes, I do and I know that it is in the country. That is exactly what I want," the guy said.

"But how can you take it over the phone without seeing it?" the landlord asked.

"My dad can come out to inspect it and send me photos. I will take his word as to whether he likes it or not," the man explained.

The landlord was assured that the man's father would call him to come out and look at the property. The father did indeed come out to inspect the property. He took photos and stated that he liked the place. He promised that his son would call the landlord once he received the photos. The son called a couple days later and stated that he wanted to take the place. He would pay a deposit to hold it. He would arrive a week later and pay the first month's rent. The landlord also requested that he go ahead and sign the lease, as other people had expressed interest in the property. The man signed the emailed lease and faxed it back to the landlord. The father met the landlord and paid the deposit in cash. The landlord wrote on the receipt that the deposit was non-refundable since he was holding the property. It appeared to be a done deal. However, weeks went by and the man didn't arrive from California. The landlord called him and was given several excuses for the delay: first the man's income tax check was delayed and finally he wasn't going to get a check due to a tax audit. But he promised he was still coming and going to move in. Two weeks later, the man shows up on the property without calling the landlord. He pulled up on the secluded private tract of land in a U-Haul pulling a car. The property is located in such a way that you need to be familiar on how to get in and out. Once the man realized that, he called the landlord. The man had driven onto private property that was difficult to maneuver his truck into. He couldn't turn around in the drive-way because the road was too narrow.

"We are here from California," he told the landlord when he called him.

"Where are you?" the landlord asked, puzzled.

"We are on your property right now."

The landlord rushed to his car to go to his property. He found the man, his wife and child waiting on him near dark at night. He could hear dogs barking in the back of the U-Haul.

"Why didn't you call me before you drove here? It's almost dark and we won't be able to see the property," the landlord explained.

"We got here this morning but decided to visit family first." That was the landlord's first red flag that something wasn't right. Why would anyone drive to a property near dark and not call the landlord first? Why were dogs in the truck?

"Well, let's go inside," the landlord told them as they walked to the house. The man's wife was the first to speak as they all looked around. She was not happy with what she saw.

"This will never do. I have asthma and it feels moist in here," she said.

"The heat is down low since the place is vacant. I will raise the heat," the landlord said.

"No, no, I don't like it. Look, I see cobwebs up there. What kind of place is this?" the lady asked, nervously looking around. They had previously lived in a stucco townhouse in an urban city in California. This home and its North Carolina country setting were totally different.

"What do you mean, what kind of place is this?' the landlord asked.

"The house doesn't look like houses in California. It looks different," she replied.

"Your father-in-law sent you photos," the landlord said.

"This is a double-wide mobile home," her husband told her.

"I've never seen a house like this," she complained as she stepped outside.

"These homes are common in this part of the country," her husband explained.

"I don't want it and I don't want to stay here," she said, walking outside. Their small child was banging things all around in the kitchen and was doing his best to break something.

The landlord looked in disapproval at the kid, seeing that the parents weren't paying attention.

"Honey, are you sure? We already signed the lease and paid the deposit," the man tried to convince his wife.

"No, I am not staying here. He needs to give our money back," she said.

"Your deposit is non-refundable because I turned other people away," the landlord told her.

"Come on, man, have a heart. Refund our money. She doesn't like it," the man said.

"I can't because I held it for three weeks. Other people could have moved in," the landlord said cautiously. He had turned down several prospective tenants since these people had paid a deposit.

"Have a heart. We are broke. We don't even have money for a hotel room," the man said.

"What do you mean you don't have money? How were you going to pay me the rent?" the landlord asked, getting angry.

"We thought we would get the rent from family members and that you would let us stay until we got the rent money," the man said.

"So you were going to stay for free?" the landlord said, getting mad.

"We were going to stay for a couple days."

"Well, we're finished. Since you refuse to honor the lease, I certainly am not going to refund a deposit," the landlord said.

"You have to refund the deposit. We don't have money for a hotel. Where can we stay?" The man kept on and on about not having a place to sleep, especially for his child. The landlord, against his better judgment decided to give them back $100.

"I'll give you $100 back so that you can get a hotel for the night," he told them.

The couple reluctantly went back to the big truck to leave. They still wanted to argue about getting the full deposit back. The man had backed the truck up into a field. It had been raining the day before and the land was still wet. As he tried to move forward, he got stuck in the field. His tires wouldn't move in the thick wet mud. He spun his tires over and over.

"You should have never driven on the property without calling me first," the landlord said.

"This is your fault. This is your property and you need to get me out of here," the man said.

The man continued to grind the tires into the mud as the evening got darker and darker. The landlord went and got his tractor and a chain to try to pull the man out of the mud. He spent around an hour trying to pull the truck out of the mud. The kid was misbehaving the whole time and the 2 dogs were still in the U-Haul. It would have been enough to challenge any man's patience.

"It's not going to work. I have already bent a piece on my tractor. You need to call a tow truck," the landlord told the man.

"I can't pay for a tow truck. I don't have any money," the man replied.

"I just gave you $100."

"I need that for the hotel. You need to pay for the tow truck since this is your property."

"I can't believe you drove from California without money and planned on staying here for free," the landlord said, getting very mad.

"That's why I want my deposit back. I need money," the man continued to argue.

"Look, I have been here for four hours. You had no intention of paying me. You want me to give you money?" the landlord said, looking at his watch to see the time.

"I want you to pay for towing," the man continued to argue.

"Here is the number of a towing truck company," the landlord said, giving him a phone number.

"I can't pay for it. So I'm not leaving." The family walked to the big U-Haul and got in.

The landlord had been with the man for around 4 hours by then and it was almost 10:00 at night. He went back to his car and phoned the local sheriff. He explained the situation to the sheriff. The sheriff had to come out to tell the man to leave and that he couldn't stay on private property. The landlord left assuming that the people had left. The next morning, they were gone but they had left giant tire tracks on the property. The deep ruts had to be filled with dirt. Not only did the landlord not get his rent, but he also had the expense of paying to fill up the tire ruts on his property. The lease was useless and he had lost the other prospective tenants. Not meeting the tenant in person had a really bad outcome for the landlord. If he had met them, he never would have rented the place to them. He didn't know anything about the dogs or the misbehaving child. You have to screen the tenants in person before signing the lease!

Also you should make sure that you meet everyone who will be living in the rental. If the prospective tenant has a family, meet all of the members including the kids. The way the kids behave may provide insight into how the household is run. If the kids are in control of the household, they could be pretty destructive. There will be kids who color all the rooms in the house with crayons and the parents are ok with it. Also, find out about any potential problems that the tenant may have. There are tenants who like to drink, party and do drugs. There are all kinds of lifestyles that the landlord needs to know about. If their teen-agers speak about having lots of friends over for the weekend, think about whether it's a good idea to rent to them. Try to pick up on what kind of lifestyle your tenant lives. Everyone likes to relax and enjoy the weekend but do you want a 'party animal' living in your property? Bonfires? Beer cans on the front lawn? Learn to trust your instincts about people. If something doesn't seem right, you need to think about it before you sign the lease. First impressions are usually valid.

ALWAYS MEET YOUR PROSPECTIVE TENANTS!

TIRE RUTS LEFT BY A TENANT

CHAPTER 3:
CHECK ALL EMPLOYMENT, CREDIT, BACKGROUND REFERENCES

Do not take their word that they have excellent credit or have been on the job for years. Tenants don't always tell the truth. Sometimes they "fudge" their rental application. Their income may not be as high as they claim, their credit score may be low and their references could actually be their relatives. Calling relatives for references is not a good idea. Have you ever heard a mother say her son is a low life? It just isn't going to happen. You need solid work references, business associates and the references of previous landlords. Speaking with their present and former landlords is crucial. Most are more than willing to give an honest opinion of their former tenants. They will tell you how much damage was done to their property, how much rent is still owed and if they had to evict them. If the tenant told you how bad their landlord was, use caution. Was the landlord actually bad or were they bad tenants? Tenants who don't pay their rent never like the landlord. The work reference will provide you with needed information such as whether or not the tenant is responsible and goes to work every day. If the tenant has been with the same company for a long time, they must be a good worker who is responsible. If the rental application shows that the tenant has had six jobs within the year, a red flag should go up. Something is clearly wrong and they may lose their current job after they move into your property. They may also have a low credit score. People who rent may not have the resources to own a home but this doesn't always mean that they can't afford your property. Sometimes they just don't make enough money to have acquired a good credit history. But on the other hand, a low score can show that they have too many bills based on what they earn, which means they could also be a risk of not paying the rent. When the economy is bad, you may have to make a few exceptions. Maybe the tenant has lost a job and now has a job that pays much less. Maybe they had a medical condition which ruined their credit. Ask questions about why the score is low. Maybe you will still be comfortable renting to them if they are honest about why the score is low. The following story illustrates how you need to carefully screen your tenants. Even if the tenant appears to be perfect and has plenty of cash, you still need to proceed with caution!

THE LAWSUIT HAPPY TENANT

The landlord had a very nice property in a golf course community. He had worked really hard in remodeling the place. The landlord had put in new wood flooring, painted every room, remodeled the bathrooms and installed new kitchen appliances. The place looked spectacular so the landlord was going to be very careful about who he chose as a tenant. The landlord intended to screen very carefully. He received many applicants over the course of a few months but none were fully qualified. However, one day, a prospective tenant emailed the landlord about the property. The applicant was a single middle-aged woman who owned her own business. She was divorced, had grown children and didn't have pets. All the information seemed great so the landlord immediately made arrangements to show the place to the woman. She appeared to be the perfect tenant for this property.

"I loved the place as soon as I entered," the woman told the landlord as they walked through the newly remodeled townhouse.

"Is it too much space for you?" the landlord asked, pleased that she liked it.

"Oh no, I have lots of furniture and big room size rugs. It is perfect."

The landlord thought he had found his perfect tenant. So he handed her the application along with the sheet for references.

"Just fill out the application along with your references and fax it back to me," the landlord advised, thinking that his place was rented to the right tenant.

"Oh, I am so excited that I will fill it out right here," she told the landlord.

The landlord waited while the applicant completed the application.

"I can pay you the deposit and 2 months rent right now today," the lady offered.

"You want to pay today?" the landlord asked in disbelief.

"Yes, I have the money with me. I need a place to live," she said.

"I will need to check your employment and references and get back with you tomorrow," the landlord said. Tenants usually don't offer to pay before their references are checked out.

"We can't do it today?" she asked counting $100 bills from her purse. The landlord's wife was with him and shook her head 'no' at her husband.

"I'm sorry but I have to check your references" he explained.

"Well, all right but I'm anxious to pay you," the woman said, not wanting to leave and waving the bills in the air, not wanting to put them back in her purse. They shook hands and the landlord took the application with him so that he could make his calls. He and his wife discussed it as they left. They both knew that something wasn't quite right. They both had a gut feeling about the woman. Something didn't add up.

"Why was she so anxious to pay without us checking her references, something didn't feel right," the landlord's wife told him.

"We'll check her out as soon as we get to the office," he agreed.

Upon getting to his office, he immediately began making calls. The applicant was self- employed but rented an office space. He called her business landlord first to verify that she was a business owner and what type of tenant she was.

"Hello, I'm Mr. Smith and I'm calling in regards to Ms. Jones," he told the other man.

"Yes, Ms. Jones does have a space in my building. She does graphic arts and works from this office. She has been here for around 6 months. She moved from another location," he explained pausing as he spoke.

"Does she pay her rent on time?" the landlord asked.

"Well she is paying on time but…." he began nervously.

"Oh, what is the problem?" the landlord asked, worried.

"I shouldn't be telling any of this. But I feel like I have an obligation to tell you. But if you tell anyone that I said it, I will deny it," he began.

"What is it? Please tell me," the landlord said.

"This lady is someone that you should be careful of. I found out that she has 5 law- suits pending against business associates and her last landlord. I didn't know it when I leased to her. If I had known it, I would not have signed a lease with her. She handed me cash before I checked her references," he explained.

"That is exactly what she tried to do with me. She tried to get me to take cash and pay before I checked her references," the landlord told him.

"You are lucky. You got out in time. This lady is lawsuit happy. I'm afraid of her," the man said.

"I really appreciate your honesty. I can't thank you enough," the landlord said.

"I hope that I don't get in trouble with her. At least I saved you," the man laughed.

The landlord did get lucky. Thanks to the honesty of the landlord reference, he was saved a lot of agony and problems. He could have easily been another of the lady's victims. So always trust your instincts. If something doesn't seem right, it probably isn't right. The landlord's wife picked up on it. Do not make hasty decisions. Take the time to think things over. Steady job, enough income and good references are the key elements in making the decision to rent to someone. Flashing cash at the landlord should be a red flag that the tenant doesn't want their references or credit checked. Most people write a check or use a cashier's check. If the landlord had taken the money and let her sign the lease, he would probably have ended up in small claims court — or worse. Her anxious behavior was a definite clue that she was desperate to rent the place. If a tenant appears too desperate, it's possible that no one else will rent to them. It can't be stressed enough that the landlord must check with the previous landlord. If you cannot get in contact with that landlord for a reference, wait before you sign your lease. In addition to that, it is a good idea to actually drive to the prospective tenant's residence to check it out. If you don't like what you see, you may not want to rent to that person. Your property will look the same as their present residence.

CHECK OUT REFERENCES BEFORE TURNING OVER THE KEYS

SAMPLE RENTAL APPLICATION

* Applicant must be 18 or older
* There is a non-refundable fee of $20.00 per adult to apply

Applicant's Name: Last_____ First_____ Middle_____

Social Security #_____ Driver's License#_____

Home Phone:_____ Cell Phone:_____ Work Phone:_____

All other Occupants: Relationship to Applicant

_____   _____

_____   _____

All Pets Listed with their type and breed:

_____ _____ _____

EMPLOYMENT HISTORY

Present Employment:_____ Address:_____

Phone Number:_____

Dates of Employment:_____

Monthly or Weekly Gross Pay:_____

Previous Employment:_____ Address:_____

Phone Number:_____

Dates of Employment:_____

List any other form of income:_____ Income Amount:_____

RENTAL HISTORY:

Present Address:_____ Landlord's Phone Number:_____

Rent Amount Paid:_____

Reason for leaving:_____

Was rent always paid on time?_____ Did you give a notice to leave?_____

Were the utilities in your name?_____ Were you asked to leave?_____

Have you ever been evicted?_____

Explanation for answers:_____

_____

_____

CREDIT HISTORY

Bank Account Name: _____

Checking Account: _____

Savings Account: _____

Credit Card: _____

CAR LOANS/LOANS

Vehicles: Own, lease or making payments? _____

Model: _____ Make: _____ Year: _____ Color: _____

License Plate#_____

REFERENCES (Non-Relative)

Name:_____ Address:_____ Phone: _____

Name:_____ Address:_____ Phone: _____

EMERGENCY CONTACT

Name:_____ Address:_____ Phone: _____

GENERAL INFORMATION

Have you ever been served a late rent notice?_____

How long do you plan on renting this property?_____

Have you been served an eviction notice?_____

Will you or other occupants be smoking in this property?_____

Are you presently involved in a lawsuit? Have you ever been involved in a lawsuit?_____

If yes, please explain.

Do you have a criminal record?_____ Felony?_____ Misdemeanor?_____

When we run a credit check and criminal background, will there be anything negative found?_____

AGREEMENT AND AUTHORIZATION

I believe that the statements I have made are true and accurate. I hereby authorize a credit and/or criminal background check to be made on me. I give permission to communicate with the contacts and references that I have listed on this application. I understand that this is an application and doesn't constitute an actual lease agreement. The $20.00 fee is non-refundable and covers the cost of processing my application. I am not entitled to a refund if I don't get the rental property.

Signature:_____ Date:_____

RENTAL TOWNHOME

CHAPTER 4:
THE TENANT MUST DO A WALK-THROUGH INSPECTION

This rule will help the landlord avoid any future problems with "he said, she said" types of situations. If the tenant sees a problem with the property, the inspection will give them a chance to point it out. The landlord should have a list prepared and check each item and then have the tenant initial the item that they have read it.

SAMPLE INSPECTION CHECKLIST
1. Exterior yard is free of trash and debris.
2. The grass around the property is cut and trimmed.
3. The front door bell is in working order.
4. The outside lights are in working order.
5. The exterior doors are all in working order.
6. The garage door is in working order.
7. The interior walls are in good condition (no crayon, holes or obvious blemishes).
8. The flooring is in good condition (carpet has been cleaned, no obvious tears or rips in the carpet or vinyl, no loose hardwood or laminate).
9. All appliances that are being left as part of the rental are in working order.
10. All toilets and sinks are in working order (no leaks).
11. All interior lights are in working order.
12. There are no broken windows or windows that won't open.
13. The heat and A/C units are in working order.
14. Smoke detectors and/or carbon monoxide units are installed and in working order.
15. There are no obvious safety hazards.

The landlord can make the list of items specific to the property, for example, if you have a patio, deck or pool etc. It is advisable not to rent a property with a pool. The landlord will assume too much liability and safety issues. The tenant may not use caution with the pool with their family and/or guests. The tenant also may not do proper maintenance to the pool and it can become another expense for the landlord. The landlord may have to deal with pool accidents as well as pool maintenance. So it would be highly recommended to not rent a property with a pool. If it has an above ground pool, take it down. If it's a regular in-ground pool, cover it up so that it can't be used.

Make sure that the tenant initials each item on your list. This way you can pull it out if they complain about something. Also, when they move, you will take out the list and compare. If you have to go to court, you will have the list. Make any notes that are needed on the list. If something does need repair, note it and state when you will fix it. After you fix it, have the tenant sign off on it. If you end up with walls that are colored with crayons when the tenant moves, your list will state that the walls were not colored with crayon before they moved in. If the tenant sees any problems or anything that needs repair, now is their chance to speak up. They may point things out that you aren't willing to fix or repair. Maybe the carpet isn't clean enough to suit the tenant. You have to decide if you are willing to clean it again or if the tenant will have to decide if they are willing to accept it as it is. If they accept it, then they can't complain later. Many times at a court hearing for evictions, the tenant will use the excuse that the property wasn't habitable or something was wrong with it. Almost every time, the judge will ask the tenant, "Why did you choose to live there if it was so bad?" That's an excellent question. Why would the tenant sign a lease if the property was horrible? If the landlord has done the walk through, there is your proof that the tenant saw the property and was fine with it. Nothing more can be said if the landlord hands the judge the inspection sheet. You will also take photos along with the list. This will be your best protection against damages. There is nothing better than to have before and after photos. It will serve you well if you need to collect damages from the tenant. Comparing before and after photos is the best proof that you can collect. If the tenant claims that their pet didn't tear the carpet, pull out the dated photo of how the carpet looked before they moved in. You can be almost certain that if you go to court, the judge will ask to see before and after photos if the claim is disputed. If the landlord is leaving any items in the property, note them as well (for example, if the landlord is providing blinds, drapes, appliances, or furniture used for staging). It will be the landlord's word against the tenant's if the tenant decides to take the landlord's possessions when they leave.

TAKE PHOTOS OF EVERYTHING!

FURNISHED CONDO

CHAPTER 5:
THE LANDLORD MUST VERIFY WHO WILL BE LIVING IN THE PROPERTY

Make sure that you know exactly who will be living in the place and spell out in the lease what will happen if any new people move in. On the lease, put all the names of the people who will be living in the house. State that no one else is allowed. If you don't list the people you're allowing, it wouldn't be unusual to go from three people to ten people once the lease is signed.

JIM AND HIS EXTENDED FAMILY AND FRIENDS

Jim and his wife needed a place to live. They appeared to be hard-working folks who just didn't make a whole lot of money. Jim cleaned carpets for a living. He worked for a cleaning company who seemed to be very busy with customers. Larry worked hard and often worked late hours each day. The day that he came to look at the rental property, he could barely walk due to bursitis in his knees. Working on his knees was not easy for a middle-aged man and his knees were swollen.

"I need an affordable place to live for my family. I have a wife and 3 kids. We are quiet people who prefer to live in the country," he told the landlord.

"How old are your kids and where do they go to school?" the landlord asked.

"My kids are all teen-agers and attend the high school down the street," he told the landlord.

"Do you have any pets?"

"We have one old dog that stays outside."

"I require a pet deposit for any indoor animals."

"Well my dog prefers to be outside."

"Who will be living in the house?" the landlord asked.

"My wife, me and 2 kids."

The landlord prepared the lease and the guy and his wife signed it. The lease stated that there would be 4 people, the man, his wife and their 2 kids. Well, before long, the landlord noticed more teen-agers. He saw at least 4 coming and going on the school bus. The kids had pierced ears and tattoos.

"Who are those kids coming and going to your house each day?" he asked the tenant.

"Oh, those are my wife's kids from her previous marriage."

"Well, they can't stay at the house. They aren't part of the lease," the landlord told him.

"Don't worry, this is temporary. You won't see them much longer," he told the landlord.

Soon after, the landlord saw the police going to the house. He asked the police what was going on at his property. The police told him that there were 2 run-away teens staying at the house and he had been notified to pick them up. The landlord went down to his property to check things out.

"What is going on with the police?" he asked the tenant.

"Well, those teens need to go back home. The law said that they can't stay. They need to go back to their father." The landlord knew that the tenant was lying and acting like there wasn't a problem when in fact, the kids had left home from another state and the tenant should have reported that they were with him. He could have easily gotten in trouble with the law.

The landlord must keep track of who is coming and going to the property. If you see new people, you must check it out. Before you know it, they will be moved in and it will be difficult to get them out of your property. Tenants like to move people in during night time hours.

MOVING OTHER PEOPLE IN

Another situation arose from a couple who moved the wife's father in. The wife had an elderly father in his seventies. They didn't tell the landlord or get approval to add him to the lease. The landlord saw the man and was ok with the woman's father living with them. He figured it was her father and he needed personal care so he said nothing. Little did he know that it would be used against him in the future. The couple was getting the father's social security checks in lieu of taking care of him. Yet, they started getting behind in their rent payments. The landlord didn't understand why they were behind. He sent them notice after notice that they were late in rent. The tenants did not respond to the notices. The landlord finally confronted them about not paying rent and they admitted that they had bills and couldn't pay the rent. A lot of times, tenants will pay their car payments before they will pay their rent. This was the case with this couple and the fact that the wife didn't work. They had too many bills to keep up with. They refused to leave the house even though they were 3 months behind. The landlord gave the tenants written notice to leave due to non-payment of rent and he also filed eviction papers in court. The day of court arrived and the couple showed up. The landlord presented his case to the local judge. The couple didn't say too much because they knew they were behind in rent. The judge quickly ruled in the landlord's favor and told the couple that they had to move due to eviction. The landlord knew that they would do all kinds of damage in the meantime. The landlord tried to get into his property during those days but he couldn't because the tenants called the sheriff on him. They told the sheriff that they were moving and that the landlord was disrupting their move.

The landlord was only able to inspect his property when they left. The damages were incredible. The tenants left old furniture and trash was left inside and outside. The carpet was ruined from animal stains and several litter boxes were left filled with feces. In the kitchen drawers, there were hundreds of mice droppings. There hadn't even been minimal house-keeping. The landlord ended up with thousands of dollars in damages and non-payment of rent.

There was another situation where the landlord had a single mom living in their home for years. She paid her rent on time for several years with no problems. Suddenly she lost her job as a restaurant manager. Somehow, she still managed to come up with the rent. Then all of a sudden, the landlord saw new people at her place. The landlord saw 2 men and a woman coming and going from the house.

"Who are the people at your house?" he asked the tenant.

"Well, my sons just got out of the military. The one son has a wife. They didn't have a place to go and they don't have jobs. I told them that they could stay with me temporarily," she explained.

"But your lease states that you can't move in new people without my approval," the landlord told her.

"It will just be temporary. They need to find jobs. I just got back on my feet with a new job. I promise it won't be long, she told the landlord.

Well, the 'temporary' turned into almost a year. The 2 young men from the military weren't able to find jobs for that long. The wife of one of the men made no effort to find work. Plus, they brought pets with them. The household went from one single woman to 2 women, 2 men and 5 dogs. The landlord was stuck in the middle.

Should he evict? Should he cut his losses? What kind of damages have they done? Should the rent be increased with more people in the house? These are the types of situations that come up regularly for landlords. It can be a tough call. The landlord doesn't want to be cruel and heartless but they also don't want to be taken advantage of either. The rental property can go from 5 people living in it to having 10 or more people living in it. Some tenants like to cut their expenses by sharing them with roommates but they don't want to pay the landlord more. Extra people mean lots more wear and tear on your property.

MY DAUGHTER JUST NEEDS A CHANCE

Another case involved a mother who was searching to find a place for her adult daughter to live. The daughter was in her mid-30s and was on disability. She received a monthly check from the state for this disability.

"My daughter needs a small place to live. She is living with me but she wants to be out on her own," the mother explained to the landlord.

"Where does she work and can she afford it?" the landlord asked.

"She doesn't work. She gets a monthly disability check for $1,400," the mother said. The landlord is thinking that $1,400 a month is enough income to cover his $450 rent.

"Well, she will have to sign a lease for the place. Since she doesn't have a landlord reference, I can make the lease for just 6 months," the landlord told her. The mother seemed quite pleased that the landlord was going to let her adult daughter have the place. The landlord never questioned what the disability was thinking that it would be awkward to ask about. So he drew up a 6 month lease and had the mother sign it for the daughter. The daughter moved into the small apartment. They fixed it up nicely and she kept it very neat and clean. The daughter kept the place immaculate. All seemed well to the landlord. But shortly after she moved in, he began to get calls from the tenant.

"There is a mouse in the place. You have to come and get it," she cried to the landlord.

"This apartment is in the country. Mice are out in the country. You need to set a trap for it," he explained.

"I have never seen a mouse in my mother's house. I'm afraid. I can't stay here until you catch it," she continued to cry.

"I will go and buy some traps and set them up at your place," the landlord told her, slightly annoyed. He figured that she was afraid of mice and that it was no big deal. The woman spent the night with her mother while the traps were set out. She only came home once the mouse was caught.

That was not the end of the landlord's problems with this tenant. More calls continued to come in on a daily basis from the tenant and her mother.

"There are fleas in the place. You need to come and fix it," she told him one day.

"You have a dog. He is causing the fleas. You need to treat him," he told her getting angry as he noticed fleas on her small dog.

"My dog doesn't have fleas. They are coming from outside. I need them gone," she cried. The landlord was beginning to suspect that something was really wrong with this woman.

He called her mother and explained the situation. The mother told him that she would go and buy flea treatment for the dog. The landlord thought that was it with all the problems. But problems continued on a regular basis. The woman didn't work and appeared to occupy her time by calling the landlord to have something to do. The landlord was beginning to question what was wrong with the woman. One day, he was busy at work but continued to get call after call from the woman. He finally stopped taking the calls and let her calls go to voicemail.

"You are a filthy landlord. You brought rats into my place" she said on the voicemail.

"You are a dirty rat, you put me into a dirty place," another voicemail stated.

The landlord tried to contact her mother but the mother was at work. The ugly voicemails continued throughout the day. Later in the day, he looked out his office window to see the woman walking down the road. She was staggering as she walked. She continued to walk to a neighbor's home. She sat down on their front steps with a drink in her hand. She was talking loudly to herself. The landlord walked down the road to see what was happening.

"You are a dirty landlord. I have rats and fleas in my place. I want to leave," she cried as she continued to talk to herself. The landlord took the drink from her hand and smelled it. It was an alcoholic drink of some type. The landlord assumed that she was drunk.

"I'm going to call your mother," he told the woman.

The woman became outraged and screamed hysterically. She began to jump up and down, screaming. She was having some type of fit and wouldn't stop. The landlord dialed the police. The woman had some kind of hysterical fit as the landlord waited for the police to arrive. When the police arrived, the woman continued to have the fit. She was jumping up and down.

"Ma'am, what are you drinking? Are you on some kind of medication?" he asked her.

"I just went to the doctor yesterday and he changed my medication. I am on medication for schizophrenia," she told him.

"Do you know anything about her being on medication for mental illness?" the police asked the landlord.

"I didn't know a thing about it until now. She has been acting strangely for a while. She has been calling me repeatedly and leaving ugly messages" the landlord explained.

"She needs to get to the hospital. She must be having a reaction to her medicine," the policeman said. With that statement, the woman became more hysterical.

"Call my momma. I want my mommy. I won't go to the hospital," she cried. The landlord took out his phone and dialed the mother. Fortunately she answered.

"Don't send her to the hospital, I'll be right over," the mother said. The landlord and policeman waited for almost an hour for the mother to arrive.

"What is wrong with your daughter?" the policeman immediately asked the mother.

"She is diagnosed as a schizophrenic and takes medicine to control it," the mother said.

"Why didn't you tell me that?" the landlord asked.

"Would you have rented to her?" she said.

"I needed to know. She could have hurt herself badly. No one would have known what to do," he said.

"I'll take her home and let her sleep. I'll bring her back in a little while," the mother said.

"No, you won't. I'm not going to be responsible for her," the landlord said.

"But she has a lease with you. You have to let her stay," the mother argued.

"She can only stay if you are with her," the landlord told her.

The mother angrily took her daughter and they left. The mother stayed with the daughter for the rest of the month. The mother thought that she would be able to get away with not revealing her daughter's medical condition. Fortunately for the landlord, it was resolved without someone getting hurt. The tenant could have seriously hurt herself or someone on the property.

Know up front who will be living in your property. It is a shame that the woman had a mental condition but the landlord should have known about it, especially if she were a risk to herself or others. The same applies to anyone who lives alone and has a medical condition. Also add a clause about moving new people in. If someone isn't listed on the lease, they need to go! If the landlord isn't comfortable about people staying overnight at the residence, that should be added too. The landlord needs to know who is staying in the property. If someone is staying more than a couple of weeks, they may have moved in. That can be added to your lease. Anyone staying over whatever time frame you have on the lease is considered a resident.

KNOW WHO IS LIVING IN YOUR PROPERTY

CHAPTER 6:
DO YOU ALLOW PETS?

List the type of pets and their names on the lease!

This is a tricky situation. The tenant will tell you that they have 1 dog. You will go to the property and you will see 2 or 3 dogs. They will make excuses like they are pet sitting or the animals are temporary. The tenants own all the animals. Animals come in the night on a regular basis or the family adopts a new pet that they just can't live without. But yet the landlord is forgotten. They may have paid a pet deposit for 1 animal but end up with 5 animals. You must get a pet deposit but establish ground rules for additional pets. You may want to add to the lease that it is grounds for eviction to add new pets without approval. Remember that although we all love our pets, pets do damage. Pets are usually responsible for most of the property damage. We have had cases where the dog chewed all the baseboards up in the rooms. Dogs have made holes in the sheetrock. The front and back doors have been destroyed from the dog scratching them trying to get out. Carpet has been torn to shreds. Pets do have accidents. Even meticulous housekeepers have to stay on top of pet accidents. Cat urine odor is particularly hard to remove. You may think your pets are angels but look underneath the carpet where a pet lives. The padding will always have stain marks from where the pet had an accident. Do you believe that your tenant will clean the carpets regularly? Be prepared to always clean the carpet when a tenant moves out. If you aren't comfortable with that, you may want to remove all carpeting and have wood, laminate or vinyl floors installed. However, pets do have the ability to ruin those floors too. So you really have to consider if you want to allow pets.

What kinds of pets? We had tenants who decided to bring in rabbits.

Those rabbits lived in the bathroom sinks. When the tenants left, the sinks were stopped up with rabbit feces, not to mention the stench. Ferrets are popular too. Do you know what kind of smell a ferret can create? You might want to think about that pet carefully. How do you feel about snakes? Sure, snakes stay in an enclosed aquarium. But what happens when it gets loose? It can take days to find them or you may never find them. If the tenant moves and they leave their lost snake, how will the new tenants feel when they find it? There was an incident where a snake climbed through a hole in the bedroom closet. Guess who found it? The next tenant! The tenant was in their bedroom getting ready to go to bed and felt that something was watching them. They looked over to find a black snake sitting on the bedroom chair. They jumped out of bed and picked up the chair with the snake. They threw the snake and chair out the front door. The tenant thought that they had solved the problem. Wrong! The next night, the snake returned through the closet. There it was again. This time the tenant took more drastic action. They took a shovel and killed the snake. They didn't want to take any chances on it returning again.

Some tenants also like to leave their pets. There was an incident where the tenant moved out and left their cat. The cat was around 10 years old. The next tenant was kind and continued to feed it. Eventually, all the people who moved in began to feed the cat. So the cat kept getting fed by those tenants. But when the house was finally vacant; the cat had no one to feed it. The landlord found the poor cat hungry and malnourished. He fed the cat and it became his cat. He kept the cat for another 10 years until it died.

There was another tenant who had 2 big dogs. When he moved, he decided to leave the dogs at the property. The dogs were naturally afraid and took refuge in a big barn on the property. The landlord didn't realize that the dogs were in the barn until one of the dogs came down to the landlord's office seeking food. The landlord began to feed the dog every day. But he wondered why the dog would carry some of the food in its mouth back to the barn. Finally the landlord went down to the barn and found the other dog. The dog had been taking food back to the other dog because it was so afraid. The dog was hungry and fearful. Once again, the landlord had to adopt 2 dogs as pets. He kept the old dogs until they died. As the landlord, avoid these problems and make sure that no pets are left behind. If you find pets, what will you do? If you can't keep them, then what?

There are also problems with outdoor pets. If your tenant wants to keep their pet outside, be careful where they put it. It is not enough to just put the pet inside a fenced yard. On more than one occasion, the dog created a problem in the outdoors. The tenant called the landlord to tell them that their air-conditioning wasn't working. The landlord went out and checked on the unit inside of the house and couldn't find the problem. He went outside to check the exterior unit. That was where he found the problem. He examined the outside unit for a few minutes. Shortly thereafter, he found the problem. The dog had chewed the thermostat wires on the unit. The wires were completely chewed up.

Evidently, the dog got bored and decided to chew on the wires. So who pays for this type of problem? Does the landlord do the repair for free or charge the tenant? This is a classic example of strange situations occurring. This particular incident occurred more than one time. On the subject of outdoor pets, what about their waste in the yard? How can you be sure that the tenant will clean up after the dog? It wouldn't be unusual to find a yard full of dog waste when the tenant moves from the house. Do you want to be left cleaning up dog poop from your tenant? Another situation to consider is the neighbors. What if a tenant has pets that bother the neighbors. There was a case where a tenant lived in the upper unit of a condo. That tenant had a large dog that weighed about 100 pounds. Not only did the dog walk loudly on the floor but it barked loudly. The tenant would go to work and leave her dog on the exterior screened in porch. The dog would bark when it heard any sounds. Of course the tenant below made sounds. Whenever that lower tenant walked or moved around, the dog barked. Who is responsible for this? What is fair? Should the tenant above be allowed to have a big dog? Should that dog be allowed on the screen porch in a condo unit? These are all questions you have to ask yourself.

The landlord who had the unit below felt the tenant above was being irresponsible. She should not have put the dog on the exterior of the condo knowing that it would bark. That landlord complained to the homeowners' association. They didn't take any action and said they would send her a notice about the dog barking. Well, that notice was ignored by the tenant. The lower unit tenant had to endure the barking. His rights were being infringed upon every time that dog went on the porch. The dog should have been kept inside. There possibly should have been an ordinance prohibiting this size dog in the condo units. A large dog doesn't always work in a condo due to space and no outdoor fencing. Since the homeowners' association wouldn't take action, the landlord advised his tenant on what to do. He advised him to call the police or animal control every time the dog was on the porch barking. The tenant only had to all animal control twice. The dog was no longer left on the porch. Sometimes, you have to take matters into your own hands. The upper unit tenant refused to cooperate and the homeowners refused as well. In these cases you have to figure out what will work to solve the problem.

The landlord has to consider pets in regards to the neighbors just as in the case of the barking condo dog. Even in neighborhoods with regular houses, pets can create problems. There was a situation where the neighbor's dog liked to escape from the fenced in backyard. The dog continued to run into the other neighbor's yard or to cross the street. The neighbors didn't just contact the owners of the dog, they contacted the landlord as well. The landlord will be involved whenever pets are involved. It is also a good idea to not allow aquariums or any water filled apparatus. Many times, a landlord will find an aquarium that has leaked onto their hardwood floors and destroyed them. The same applies with waterbeds. Are you prepared to put in new flooring due to water damage?

Photos tell the story of what can happen with pets. Make sure that you always take photos of the damage that pets cause. As you will see from the photos, not everyone cleans the litter box on a regular basis. Not everyone keeps well-behaved pets. Some dogs like to chew on baseboards, door trim, carpet and whatever else suits them. The following photos show what tenants can leave for the landlord from their pets. This is one of the most important tips for landlords. Pets can be very destructive, use caution and put the rules in the lease!

RULES FOR PETS

PET LEFT BY TENANT

CAT LITTER LEFT BY AN EVICTED TENANT

DOG TEARS UP THE CLOSET

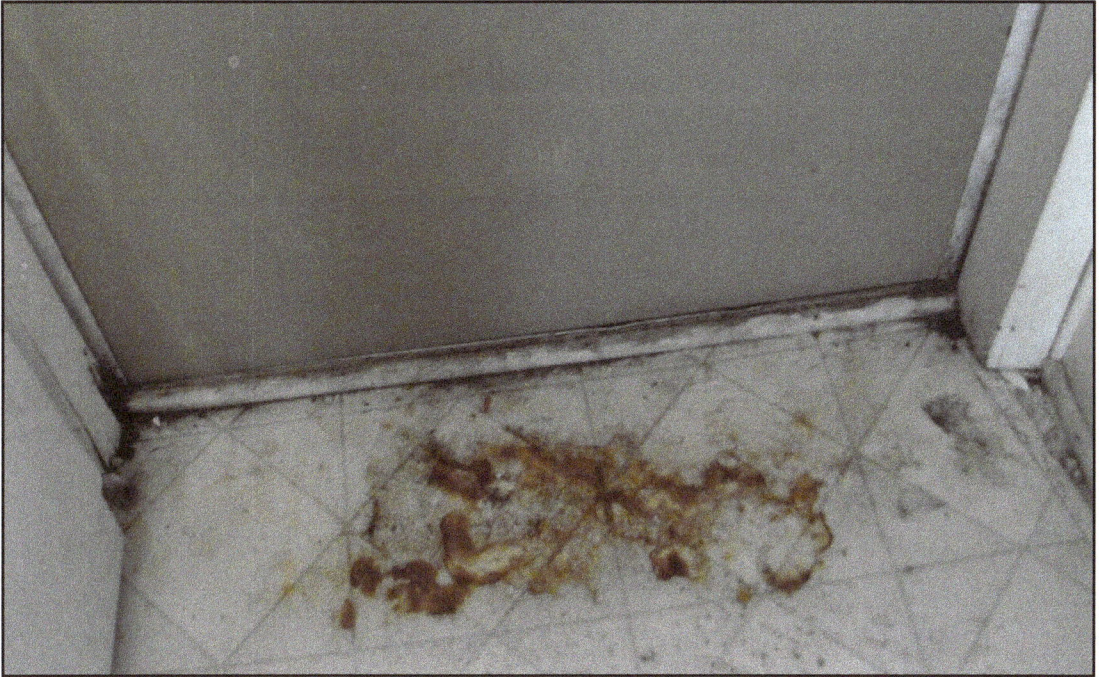

DOG DAMAGE TO THE DOOR

DAMAGE TO THRESHOLD OF DOOR

CHAPTER 7:
PREPARE THE LEASE AND INCLUDE ALL INFORMATION

Put everything you can think of in the lease to protect yourself. There are plenty of online websites that have actual leases on them you can refer to. The lease is the landlord's protection. If you need to, consult an attorney on how to do it or have them do it for you. This is your written agreement that spells everything out. You will refer to it during the lease period and you will need it for court if it ever comes to that. If the lease covers a disputed item, you will be protected in court. Also consider the length of the lease. A year's lease is typical. But sometimes a year can be a long time if the tenant isn't working out. The lease protects the tenant too. You can't just kick them out. If they sign for a year, then they stay the year provided they pay their rent and don't break rules. For tenants that you just aren't sure about, you may want to offer a month-to-month lease. This way, it can be a trial run for both of you. This might be considered for a tenant who doesn't have good credit, has never rented before or just doesn't fit the typical lease standards. With a month-to-month lease, you won't have to go through the court system if you need to do an eviction. You can just give the tenant a 7 day notice and that's it. They can also give you a notice, though. Set everything in stone. Spell it all out. Go over it several times before you give it to the tenant. Make sure that you have missed nothing. But if you do find out that you have left something out, add an addendum and have the tenant sign it. Know your state laws for what you can and cannot do. It will be worth your time and effort to know all the state laws prior to making the lease. Landlord/Tenant laws vary from state to state.

THE LEASE

1. Description of the Property (residential or commercial).
2. Names and signatures of those assuming the responsibility of the lease. List the names of all people that will be living in the house and their role in the family (husband, wife, child, etc.). Include the pets and names.
3. The length of the lease (month-to-month or yearly).
4. The amount of rent due each month.
5. The date that the rent is due.
6. What date the rent is considered late and what late fees apply (check state law on late fees).
7. The amount of the deposit.
8. The policy for the return of the deposit (do you refund it all or just a portion?).
9. A statement on the utilities being in the tenant's name(s).
10. A statement that a walk-through inspection has been done with the check list attached.
11. A statement(s) about any and all maintenance of the property.
12. Pet policy that includes description of all pets and whether a pet deposit applies.
13. A statement(s) that no one else may reside at the property other than those designated on the lease.
14. The policy on notification to the landlord for repairs.
15. The policy on loud noise, disturbances, nuisances to the neighbors. Policy on the police being called. Statement about illegal activities.
16. Statement about tenant responsibility for renter's insurance.
17. Policy on breaking the lease. What is the penalty if a tenant breaks the lease?
18. Policy on damages.
19. Policy on eviction.
20. Policy on tenant being responsible for court costs and attorney fees if a dispute goes to court.

PREPARE YOUR LEASE CAREFULLY

DESTROYED BATHROOM

SAMPLE RENTAL AGREEMENT FOR RESIDENTIAL LEASE

This Rental Agreement or Residential Lease shall evidence the complete terms and conditions under which the parties whose signatures appear below have agreed. Landlord/Lessor/Agent, _____, shall be referred to as "LANDLORD" and Tenant(s)/Lessee, _____, shall be referred to as "TENANT" As consideration for this agreement, LANDLORD agrees to rent/lease to TENANT and TENANT agrees to rent/lease from OWNER for use solely as a private residence, the premises located at

_____.

1. TERMS: TENANT agrees to pay $_____ per month on the ____ day of each month. This agreement shall commence on _____,___ and continue; until _____,___ as a leasehold. If TENANT should move from the premises prior to the expiration of this time period, he shall be liable for all rent due until such time that the Residence is occupied by a LANDLORD approved paying TENANT and/or expiration of said time period, whichever is shorter.

2. PAYMENTS: Rent and/or other charges are to be paid at such place or method designated by the owner as follows _____. All payments are to be made by check or money order and cash shall be acceptable. LANDLORD acknowledges receipt of the First Month's rent of $_____, and a Security Deposit of $_____, and additional charges/fees for _____, for a total payment of $_____. All payments are to be made payable to _____.

3. SECURITY DEPOSITS: The total of the above deposits shall secure compliance with the terms and conditions of this agreement and shall be refunded to TENANT within _30____ days after the premises have been completely vacated less any amount necessary to pay LANDLORD a) any unpaid rent, b) cleaning costs, c) key replacement costs, d) cost for repair of damages to premises and/or common areas above ordinary wear and tear, and e) any other amount legally allowable under the terms of this

agreement. A written accounting of said charges shall be presented to TENANT within _____ days of move-out. If deposits do not cover such costs and damages, the TENANT shall immediately pay said additional costs for damages to LANDLORD.

4. LATE CHARGE: A late fee of $_____, (not to exceed ___% of the monthly rent), shall be added and due for any payment of rent made after the _____ of the month.

5. UTILITIES: TENANT agrees to pay all utilities and/or services based upon occupancy of the premises. Utilities must be the TENANT'S NAME prior to moving into the premises.

6. OCCUPANTS: Guest(s) staying in the rental for more than 7 consecutive days, or a total of over 20 days in any 12 month period, is considered a resident. If done so without the written consent of OWNER shall be considered a breach of this agreement. ONLY the following individuals and/or animals, AND NO OTHERS shall occupy the subject residence for more than 20 days unless the expressed written consent of LANDLORD obtained in advance

_____.

7. PETS: No animal, fowl, fish, reptile, and/or pet of any kind shall be kept on or about the premises, for any amount of time, without obtaining the prior written consent and meeting the requirements of the LANDLORD. Such consent if granted, shall be revocable at LANDLORD'S option upon giving a 30 day written notice. In the event laws are passed or permission is granted to have a pet and/or animal of any kind, an additional deposit in the amount of $_____ shall be required along with additional monthly rent of $_____ along with the signing of LANDLORD'S Pet Agreement. TENANT also agrees to carry insurance deemed appropriate by LANDLORD to cover possible liability and damages that may be caused by such animals.

8. LIQUID FILLED FURNISHINGS: No liquid filled furniture, receptacle containing more than ten gallons of liquid is permitted without prior written consent and meeting the requirements of the LANDLORD. TENANT also agrees to carry insurance deemed appropriate by LANDLORD to cover possible losses that may be caused by such items.

9. PARKING: When and if TENANT is assigned a parking area/space on LANDLORD'S property, the parking area/space shall be used exclusively for parking of passenger automobiles and/or those approved vehicles listed on TENANT'S Application attached hereto. TENANT hereby assigned or permitted to park only in the following area or space _____. The parking fee for this space (if applicable is $_____ monthly. Said space shall not be used for the washing, painting, or repair of vehicles. No other parking space shall be used by TENANT or TENANT'S guest(s). TENANT is responsible for oil leaks and other vehicle discharges for which TENANT shall be charged for cleaning if deemed necessary by LANDLORD.

10. NOISE: TENANT agrees not to cause or allow any noise or activity on the premises which might disturb the peace and quiet of another RESIDENT and/or neighbor. Said noise and/or activity shall be a breach of this agreement.

11. CONDITION OF PREMISES: TENANT acknowledges that he has examined the premises and that said premises, all furnishings, fixtures, furniture, plumbing, heating, electrical facilities, all items listed on the attached property condition checklist, if any, and/or all other items provided by LANDLORD are all clean, and in good satisfactory condition except as may be indicated elsewhere in this Agreement. TENANT agrees to keep the premises and all items in good order and good condition and to immediately pay for costs to repair and/or replace any portion of the above damaged by TENANT, his guests and/or invitees, except as provided by law. At the termination of this Agreement, all of above items in this provision shall be returned to LANDLORD in clean and good condition except for reasonable wear and tear and the premises shall be free of all personal property and trash not belonging to LANDLORD. It is agreed that all dirt, holes, tears, burns, and stains of any size or amount in the carpets, drapes, walls, fixtures, and/or any other part of the premises, do not constitute reasonable wear and tear.

12. ALTERATIONS: RESIDENT shall not paint, wallpaper, alter or redecorate, change or install locks, install antenna or other equipment, screws, fastening devices, large nails, or adhesive materials, place signs, displays, or other exhibits, on or in any portion of the premises without the written consent of the OWNER except as may be provided by law.

13: PROPERTY MAINTENANCE: RESIDENT shall deposit all garbage and waste in a clean and sanitary manner into the proper receptacles and shall cooperate in keeping the garbage area neat and clean. TENANT shall be responsible for disposing of items of such size and nature as are not normally acceptable by the garbage hauler. TENANT shall be responsible for keeping the kitchen and bathroom drains free of things that may tend to cause clogging of the drains. TENANT shall pay for the cleaning out of any plumbing fixture that may need to be cleared of stoppage and for the expense or damage caused by stopping of waste pipes or overflow from bathtubs, wash basins, or sinks. TENANT shall do minor maintenance such as changing furnace filters, leaky faucets and all lawn maintenance unless provided by a lawn service. Lawn maintenance includes cutting, weeding and trimming.

14. HOUSE RULES: TENANT shall comply with all house rules as stated as part of this rental agreement, and a violation of any of the house rules is considered a breach of this agreement.

15. CHANGE OF TERMS: The terms and conditions of this agreement are subject to future change by LANDLORD after the expiration of the agreed lease period upon 30-day written notice setting forth such change and delivered to TENANT. Any changes are subject to laws in existence at the time of the Notice of Change Of Terms.

16. TERMINATION: After expiration of the leasing period, this agreement is automatically renewed from month to month, but may be terminated by either party giving to the other a 30-day written notice of intention to terminate. Where laws require "just cause," such just cause shall be so stated on said notice. The premises shall be considered vacated only after all areas including storage areas are clear of all TENANT'S belongings, and keys and other property furnished for TENANT'S use are returned to LANDLORD. Should the TENANT hold over beyond the termination date or fail to vacate all possessions on or before the termination date, TENANT shall be liable for additional rent and damages which may include damages due to LANDLORD'S loss of prospective new renters.

17. POSSESSION: If LANDLORD is unable to deliver possession of the residence to TENANT'S on the agreed date, because of the loss or destruction of the residence or because of the failure of the prior residents to vacate or for any other reason, the TENANT and/or LANDLORD may immediately cancel and terminate this agreement upon written notice to the other party at their last known address, whereupon neither party shall have liability to the other, and any sums paid under this Agreement shall be refunded in full. If neither party cancels, this Agreement shall be prorated and begin on the date of actual possession.

18. INSURANCE: TENANT acknowledges that LANDLORD'S insurance does not cover personal property damage caused by fire, theft, rain, war, acts of God, acts of others, and/or any other causes, nor shall LANDLORD be held liable for such losses. TENANT is hereby advised to obtain his own insurance policy to cover any personal losses.

19. RIGHT OF ENTRY AND INSPECTION: LANDLORD may enter, inspect, and/or repair the premises at any time in case of emergency or suspected abandonment. LANDLORD shall give 24 hours advance notice and may enter for the purpose of showing the premises during normal business hours to prospective renters, buyers, lenders, for smoke alarm inspections, and/or for normal inspections and repairs. LANDLORD is permitted to make all alterations, repairs and maintenance that in LANDLORD'S judgment is necessary to perform.

20. NO ILLEGAL ACTIVITIES PERMITTED ON PREMISES: These activities include any activity that is classified as unsafe and/or illegal by state or local laws. Examples: (fireworks on the premises, drug activity, public intoxication, etc.) If the police or sheriff are called to the premises due to such activity, it will result in immediate eviction. If the police or sheriff are called to the premises for any reason other than illegal activity more than two times, it will result in eviction of the tenant.

21. ASSIGNMENT: TENANT agrees not to transfer, assign or sublet the premises or any part thereof.

22. ATTORNEY FEES: If any legal action or proceedings be brought by either party of this Agreement, the prevailing party shall be reimbursed for all reasonable attorney's fees and costs in addition to other damages awarded.

23. JOINTLY AND SEVERALLY: The undersigned TENANTS are jointly and severally responsible and liable for all obligations under this agreement.

24. REPORT TO CREDIT/TENANT AGENCIES: You are hereby notified that a nonpayment, late payment or breach of any of the terms of this rental agreement may be submitted/reported to a credit and/or tenant reporting agency, and may create a negative credit record on your credit report.

25. LEAD NOTIFICATION REQUIREMENT: For rental dwellings built before 1978, TENANT acknowledges receipt of the information provided.

26. ADDITIONS AND/OR EXCEPTIONS

_____

_____.

27. NOTICES: All notices to TENANT shall be served at TENANT'S premises and all notices to LANDLORD shall be served at

_____.

28. INVENTORY: The premises contains the following items, that the TENANT may use. _____.

29. KEYS AND ADDDENDUMS: TENANT acknowledges receipt of the following which shall be deemed part of this Agreement: (Please check)
___ Keys #of keys and purposes _____
___ Pet Agreement ___ Other _____

30. ENTIRE AGREEMENT: This Agreement constitutes the entire Agreement between

LANDLORD and TENANT. No oral agreements have been entered into, and all modifications or notices shall be in writing to be valid.

31. RECEIPT OF AGREEMENT: The undersigned TENANTS have read and understand this Agreement and hereby acknowledge receipt of a copy of this Rental Agreement.

TENANT'S Signature_____Date_____

TENANT'S Signature_____Date_____

LANDLORD'S or Agent's Signature_____Date_____

List of all people who will be living in this residence:

_____

_____

List of Pets:_____

* * * * *

If any other circumstances are involved, be sure to include them on the lease. What is an illegal activity? Define illegal activity (drugs, prostitution, gambling, domestic violence, etc.). Will you allow the shooting of guns on your property? This pertains especially to landlords who have property in the country. If your property is in a country setting, what is allowed? Guns? 4-wheelers? ATVs? Outdoor bonfires? Be careful when you draw up the lease, think of all worst case scenarios!

THE TENANT WHO LIKED TO SHOOT

The landlord had several acres in the country. It was a peaceful, quiet setting away from the city. There were only 2 homes on the acreage. The landlord's brother-in-law lived in one house on 4 acres. The landlord had a tenant who was just a single man living in a small house on 3 acres. The man appeared to be a good tenant. He worked a steady job, paid his rent on time and didn't have any indoor pets. In the beginning, he was quiet and no one would know that anyone lived there if he didn't occasionally come outside.

One day in the early summer, the brother-in-law heard noise coming from outside. He realized that it was gun shots. The land was in a country setting where people would sometimes trespass and come onto the property to hunt deer. He went outside to see who was shooting on his property or nearby property. When he got to his outside porch, he saw a man running down the side of the property. The man disappeared into the woods and the gun shots stopped. He figured that whoever was shooting saw him and got scared. When that person realized that people lived in the house, they decided not to shoot on the property. He figured that it was settled and there wasn't going to be a problem. However, that was not the case. Almost every weekend, he heard the shooting. When he would go outside, the shooting would stop. Whoever was doing the shooting was doing it until he went outside. One Saturday, the brother-in-law waited to hear the gun shots. He knew approximately when the person would come each Saturday so he waited in the backyard so that he could actually see the person and catch them. As he patiently waited in the backyard, he eventually heard the gun shots. He quickly ran from the backyard.

"I'm coming out, I see you. Don't shoot," he yelled as he ran. He saw the man running toward the house next door. As he ran, he realized that it was the man who lived next door. The neighbor was the guilty party. Before he ran any further, the brother-in-law stopped at his storage building where the guy had been. He looked at his new storage building and saw bullet holes. There were at least 50 holes in the wood of the building. The neighbor had been shooting at his shed. He didn't know why the guy would shoot the building. They didn't even really know each other and only waved as they passed in the road or yard. He didn't know if he should confront the guy or not. After all, he had a gun and shooting his building wasn't exactly normal. He decided not to confront the guy. He would call his brother-in-law since it was his tenant. He knew that the guy had signed a 1 year lease for the property.

"The guy that you are renting to is shooting at my shed," he began.

"You saw him do it? Are you sure it wasn't hunters?" the landlord asked.

"It's been going on for a while. I caught him today by my shed. There are at least 50 holes in the wood," he told the landlord.

"Why would he shoot your building?" the landlord asked.

"He must be a nut. He could shoot on the property around the house. He must be shooting my building just to be stupid," he said.

"I'll have to call him and see what's going on," the landlord said.

"Do you have anything in the lease about not shooting on the property?" he asked.

"I'll have to check the lease. Since the house is in the country, I probably didn't put anything about shooting," the landlord said.

"Well check and see. If you did put something then he is in violation," he said.

"I guess just call the sheriff if he does it again. I'm going to call him and talk to him."

The landlord called the tenant as soon as he hung up with his brother-in-law.

"Are you shooting at my brother-in-law's shed? He said he saw you shoot it today," the landlord told him.

"I was out shooting on the property and accidentally shot his shed. It was just today," the tenant lied.

"He said that there are at least 50 shots in the shed. He heard shooting every weekend," the landlord told him.

"I never shot that shed. Just today, I made one or two holes, it's not a big deal," he said.

"Well, I don't want shooting on the property. It's not safe since you have a neighbor," the landlord told him.

"I moved there so that I could shoot. It's the country and I want to shoot my gun," he told the landlord angrily.

"No more shooting. It's not going to work, it's not safe," he told him.

"Well, then I may have to move," the guy said.

"You can move but you would be breaking the lease," the landlord said.

"There is nowhere in that lease that says no shooting," the tenant said.

"There might not be anything but I'm telling you," the landlord said.

The landlord and tenant argued about the shooting. Finally, the tenant said that he wouldn't shoot anymore. The landlord knew that he would have to make sure that it was part of the lease that no one could shoot on the property. He typed up an addendum for the lease that stated that a tenant could not shoot on the property. He didn't trust the tenant but at least he had him sign that he wouldn't shoot. If he did, he would be evicted. That is all that he could do to protect himself. It had never occurred to him that a tenant would shoot on his property, especially not at his brother-in-law's place.

Make sure that the lease includes everything that you can think of! You may have to add an addendum if you forget anything. Make sure that the tenant reads and signs it.

THREE THINGS TO EXPECT FROM YOUR TENANT AND THE LANDLORD MIGHT WANT THESE LISTED ON THE LEASE:

1. PAY THE RENT AND UTILITIES ON TIME
2. TAKE GOOD CARE OF THE PROPERTY
3. BE A GOOD NEIGHBOR

GUN SHELLS LEFT BY A TENANT

CHAPTER 8:
DETERMINE WHEN THE RENT AND LATE FEES ARE DUE

In North Carolina, the landlord may charge 5% of the rent for the late fee. Check state requirements on how to determine the late fees. The information provided here is based on North Carolina law and is not intended to serve as a substitute for legal advice. If you have more than 1 property that you are renting, it is better to keep everyone on the same rent pay day. This is easier for you and for your record keeping. You need to make sure that you give the tenant a receipt and keep accurate records of the rent for yourself. Most landlords collect on the first day of the month and give a grace period.

Rent is considered late after 5 days from the date due. Late fees vary from state to state. Typically, these can be anywhere from $15.00 to 5% of the rent, whichever is greater. The fee may only be charged once per month. It cannot be increased based on the number of days past the payment date. Check your state for the amount allowed. Security deposits are used for damages and any back rent owed. A landlord may keep part or all of the security deposit for: 1. Back rent owed 2. Costs for repairs of damage beyond normal wear and tear. 3. Lost rent and expenses for finding another tenant if the tenant moved before the lease ended. 4. Court costs if tenant is evicted. After the tenant moves out for any reason (including eviction) the landlord will give the tenant a written account of any items deducted from the deposit and refund the balance. The landlord has 30 days from the time the tenant moves out to give this accounting and refund. The landlord should have copies of all receipts and invoices ready with the accounting record.

Be prepared that most tenants will try to avoid paying the late fee.

They will call you and say they will be coming to pay the rent and then not show up. All kinds of excuses will be made as to why they shouldn't have to pay the late fee. Those excuses can range from they had to make a car payment, they missed work or they had to buy birthday gifts for their kids. If the landlord has a mortgage on the property and is late with a payment, they will have to pay a late fee, so the tenant needs to pay one as well. Paying the rent should be the tenant's first priority. After all, they have to have a place to live.

THE TENANT WITH ALL THE EXCUSES

The landlord had a nice townhouse to rent so he tried to be very careful in choosing who he would rent the property to. Since it was in a nice golf course community, he had a lot of applicants. There were young married couples, single moms and big families who had interest in his townhouse. Most of the applicants didn't qualify. They either had bad credit or didn't have the income. Due to this situation, the place sat vacant for quite a few months. He would rather let it sit than rent it to the wrong person. He continued to advertise it in various media sources. One day, a middle-aged woman called to see if she could come out to look at it. The landlord met her and he was pleased to find that she seemed to meet the criteria. She claimed to be a self-employed professional who recently got divorced. She had custody of 1 teenager. Her other 2 daughters were in college. The woman also got child support. But since she was divorced, she didn't have good credit. The landlord hesitated because of that.

He told her that he would need to see proof of her income. Within several days, she showed her check stubs from a job that she had in addition to her own small business. She also brought proof of the child support. The landlord once again hesitated and told her that he would get back with her.

He discussed it with his wife and they weren't sure because the woman had bad credit and her small business was slow because of the bad economy. He put off calling the woman and assumed that she would know that he didn't care to rent it to her. However, months went by and he still hadn't found a tenant. The woman called him back. She advised him that she would do whatever he needed to qualify for the place. She would give him more references or whatever was needed. The landlord took more references from her. Her references checked out fine but he still didn't feel quite comfortable. Ignoring his feelings, he decided to let her have the place since her income seemed adequate. She paid her deposit and first month's rent and moved in.

The next month he went to the property to pick up the rent and to see how things were going. The woman didn't have the rent and the property wasn't what he expected to see. The place was messy and her belongings were still not unpacked. Her college girls were living in the place, so there were 4 tenants instead of 2. He questioned her and got some excuses.

"My daughters haven't left for school yet. They are only here temporarily. My child support check is late so I don't have the rent," she explained.

"You showed me your pay stubs proving you could pay the rent without the child support" the landlord said.

"Well, there were unexpected expenses. The move cost extra and we needed things for the place" she said.

The landlord walked away with an uneasy feeling. She had all kinds of excuses. Those excuses continued the entire time she lived there. The next month she lost her job.

"I can't come up with the rent until I find a new job — bear with me," she told him.

"The third time you are late, you will be evicted as per the lease" he told her.

"I'll do better. I just need time to adjust" the woman cried.

"I'm sorry but if I don't have the rent on time next month, you will get a notice," he told her. The landlord knew that she would probably be late and he would have to evict. However, her lease just happened to end that same month. So he just wouldn't renew her lease. It was a lesson learned. If you don't get good credit references, the tenant probably won't have a credit card or other back-up to pay the rent. Also, child support should not be considered as part of the income as it is supposed to be for the child. The woman hadn't been screened carefully enough and she didn't tell the truth about who would be living in the property. Excuses don't pay the bills!

<hr>

TYPICAL EXCUSES WHY TENANTS CAN'T PAY THE RENT

1. I didn't get paid on time.
2. My car payment came due at the same time and I can't afford to pay both.
3. I didn't get my child support this month.
4. My car needed repairs.
5. I missed work and my check was short.
6. Someone owes me money and they didn't pay me.
7. My bank messed up my bank account.

<hr>

NO EXCUSES FOR NOT PAYING THE RENT!

CHAPTER 9:
THE TENANT MUST QUALIFY ON THEIR OWN WITHOUT CO-SIGNERS

If a potential tenant can't qualify to lease your property on their own, it is a red flag. After all, if they don't qualify, someone will have to assume the responsibility. This may be the case of parents signing for their children. If the adult children need a co-signer, then they probably aren't responsible or credit worthy enough to rent to. Having young adults living together doesn't always work out in the landlord's favor. Young adults may not have the experience to know how to live on their own.

THE PARTY BOYS

Three young men — all around the age of 21 — decided to live together. The landlord knew the parents of one of the young men. All of the young men had jobs that were mediocre and none of them had credit. They appeared to be responsible and hard working. The landlords said it would be ok if the parents co-signed. Remember, the young men had never lived on their own; they had only lived with their parents. Red flag! They would think it was time to do whatever they couldn't do in their parents' house. That means party, party, party and not pay the rent. The young men didn't know how to manage their money. Each month, rent was late and they didn't want to pay the late fee. Several times the police were called out by other neighbors because of the men's parties on the weekends. This should be in the lease too. Add the statement that if the police are called out twice due to the tenant creating a problem, that is grounds for eviction. Throughout all the fun of the parties, two of the men lost their jobs. That means that the rent didn't get paid. The young men seemed to like hanging around the house all day.

"I will have to go to your parents since they co-signed," the landlord told them.

"They won't be able to pay either. My dad lost his job," they said.

The landlord went to the parents but the men were right — the parents weren't in any position to pay the rent. They couldn't even pay their own rent. It was time to evict the men and the men didn't like it one bit.

"We don't want to go back home," they told the landlord.

"Well, you didn't pay the rent, so you have to."

"We will leave on Saturday morning," they said.

The landlord checked their place that day to make sure that everything was ok. He thought he was doing the right thing by inspecting it. Everything seemed in order. Wrong! That night, the young men threw a huge party. They had dozens of friends over for a farewell party. The party was huge with tons of beer. The party guests took their beer bottles and threw them all over the inside of the house. They also took a grocery store cart that they had stolen and filled it up with all their beer cans. There were at least several hundred beer cans inside the house. But that wasn't enough damage for these young men. They wanted to get really ugly with the landlord. So they took their furniture and put in on the front lawn. The front lawn was lined with a bed mattress, bed frame, sofa and odds and ends. But that wasn't enough either. They decided to set fire to it all.

"Let's burn this furniture up. It will save us moving it and teach the landlord a lesson," they all laughed as they set matches to the furniture. The furniture made a perfect bonfire for the party-goers. It quickly burned as they surrounded it while drinking their beer. But the frames of the furniture didn't burn since they were metal.

"Let's take it and throw it on the roof" the boys laughed as they picked up a sofa. The boys threw the partially burned sofa on the roof of the house. They never thought that it might set the house on fire. They were all too drunk. The party went on all night. The men only left once everything was burned up and they needed to sleep.

Thankfully, the fire burned out and the house was left standing. The men left the property totally destroyed with all the damage inside and the burned up stuff on the roof and front lawn. The landlords found the damage in the morning. In all the years of being landlord they have never seen anything like this. They are thankful only that the house wasn't burned down. The landlord called the police.

"I will take the report and you will need to file it in court," the sheriff advised, shaking his head.

"Can you arrest them?" the landlord asked.

"It's a civil matter since the house didn't burn down. You will need to press charges for damages through the court system." The landlord immediately called the young man's parent whom he knew.

"Your son has damaged my property. He nearly burned the place down and he owes 2 months rent," the landlord told them.

"Well, I can't help what he did. I just lost my job and don't have any money," the parent explained. The landlord couldn't believe that he had trusted the parent to pay the rent.

Do not accept a co-signer. They will not be able to pay for their kid's mistakes. The landlord knew that he would have to go to court and file a claim. He wouldn't get a dime because these folks have nothing. He got a judgment for taxes purposes and that is it. You can't get blood out of a turnip. It was a big mistake and a big lesson learned. The landlord will not rent to a group of irresponsible young people who cannot qualify on their own. It is a big loss with at least a couple thousand dollars in damage. The landlord had to hire a group of people that are similar to the people who go in after a contamination disaster. The men wear plastic suits and masks. The landlord took pictures before they started to clean up. He needed the photos for court. It was his word against the young men. Chances were that the young men would not appear in court. A judgment was to be issued to the landlord and that is it. The property was contaminated and who knows what is in there. No one would clean it up. The landlord made a huge mistake and had to pay for a huge mistake!

NO CO-SIGNERS!

BURNED UP FURNITURE BY THE PARTY BOYS

BEER CANS FROM THE PARTY BOYS

PARTY BOYS LEAVE THE SOFA

AFTER THE PARTY BOYS

BEFORE THE PARTY BOYS

CHAPTER 10:
DO NOT FALL FOR SOB STORIES

Remember that the tenant has a sob story for some reason or another. It is one thing to tell the landlord that they were in a medical crisis that was a setback or they were out of work for a while. But it's different when they tell you that they got behind on car payments or had to loan a friend money. If they can't handle their money, they won't be able to pay the rent.

Stories will vary from having temporary people living in the house, not being able to pay until they find a better job or until they get a settlement. Remember that they may never get that better job or settlement. If they don't, what will you do? It's hard to listen to stories of people getting sick or losing their jobs. But the longer you wait for things to change, the bigger risk you take as the landlord. One of the main excuses that a tenant may use is that their car is broken and not running. Since the car isn't running, they can't get to work. They also don't have the money to fix the car.

I CAN'T PAY THE RENT

One of the landlord's tenants got behind on his rent. The man, his wife and 2 kids had paid rent on time for over a year. Then one day, the rent was late. The next month, it was late again. The landlord made a trip to his property to see what was going on.

"You always pay on time. What's the problem?" he asked the man. The man shifted uncomfortably and ho-hummed around before he answered.

"I have missed some work. My car is not running. It konked out on me yesterday," he explained nervously.

"Well, you have to get to work. Can someone pick you up or can you borrow a car?' the landlord asked, trying to help.

"I don't know for sure. I don't have anyone to pick me up. Maybe I can borrow a relative's car," he replied.

"I have to have the rent, at least 1 month's rent" the landlord told him.

"I'll see what I can do" the man said walking away.

The landlord didn't get any rent money in the next couple of weeks. He went back to his property. When he pulled up to the property, he saw an eyesore of the man's old car up on cinder blocks. The man had removed the tires and it appeared that he had been working on it. The landlord stared at the car as the tenant came outside.

"That old car is still not running. I have missed work and don't have a way to get there" he told the landlord.

"Why are the tires off and why is it on cinder blocks?" the landlord said getting mad.

"I tried to work on it and it had a flat tire. I couldn't afford to pay anyone to fix it."

"You need to figure something out. You are going on 3 months past due. I can't have that car sitting in the yard like that. The neighbors won't like it," the landlord told him.

"I'll see what I can do," the guy said knowing that he planned on doing nothing.

"I'll be back in a couple of days. That car better be off those blocks and I better have some rent," the landlord said.

The landlord left knowing that he would have to go file eviction papers the next morning. There was no way that this guy could catch up on the rent, especially without a car. A couple of days later, the landlord went back to the tenant's place to let him know that he had filed eviction papers. As he pulled up in the drive-way, a brand new car pulled up behind him. It was the tenant driving the new car. The landlord jumped out of his car.

"Did you rent a car?" he asked, getting mad.

"No, I, uh, borrowed a car" the tenant explained, getting nervous.

"Well, I came to let you know that I filed eviction papers. You'll be getting a court summons this week," he told him.

"Well, we need to move anyways. We will find us something else," the guy said angrily.

"How will you move when you can't pay the rent here?" the landlord asked. Just then, the man's wife came out of the house. She didn't see the landlord.

"Honey, let's take a ride in our new car. Let's drive over to my mother's," she said not knowing that the landlord was standing there.

"So you bought a new car but you can't pay the rent," the landlord said.

"She meant that it was borrowed. Don't listen to her," the guy said getting nervous that he had been caught in a lie.

"I'll make sure that the judge knows about your new car when I see you in court," the landlord said as he left. The landlord couldn't believe that he fell for the man's excuse and lie. The landlord had waited too long to file those eviction papers. He knew that he should have filed them after the first month's rent wasn't paid.

The tenant had pulled a fast one. Instead of paying his rent, he bought a new car. He had never been trying to repair the old car. That was just part of his story so that the landlord would believe him. Evidently, making the car payment was more important than paying the rent.

Don't fall for excuses, lies or feeling sorry for the tenant! The longer the landlord waits, the more rent won't get paid. Once the tenant gets behind in rent, it is very difficult to catch it up to date. If the landlord sees that the rent isn't going to get paid, they need to go ahead and file for the eviction. If the tenant decides to pay, the landlord can always cancel the eviction court date. The landlord will be the loser, not the tenant.

FILE FOR EVICTION!

THE CAR THAT WAS BEING WORKED ON

JUNK CARS LEFT BY TENANT

CHAPTER 11:
DETERMINE WHO IS RESPONSIBLE FOR LAWN CARE AND MAINTENANCE

If you don't tell the tenant about cutting the grass, they may expect you to do it. Spell it out in the lease. If they don't have a lawnmower, they may need to prepare to get one. If they don't cut the grass, who is going to do it? It will be the landlord or a lawn service. If a lawn service or the landlord does cut the grass, state in the lease that the tenant must pay for it. The landlord can state in the lease about lawn maintenance and what will occur if the lawn isn't cut. State the price of the lawn service or the price that you, the landlord, will charge. When the tenant gets the bill, they shouldn't be surprised. Do you as the landlord want to be called every time there is a minor problem? There are tenants who will call the landlord to change the light bulb. Those tenants will state that they don't want to be responsible. If you don't want to be called for minor repairs, put it in the lease. Minor repairs could include changing light bulbs, changing furnace filters, changing ice maker filter, fixing a leaky faucet. Determine what is minor and is fair for the tenant to be responsible for. Put it in the lease agreement. The landlord on the other hand needs to be responsible for major repairs and maintenance. If the roof starts leaking, the landlord is responsible. If the heating and air-conditioning go out, the landlord is responsible. If something less urgent occurs that needs repair, the landlord has 30 days to repair or replace it.

The landlord doesn't need to put themselves in the predicament of fixing very minor things that the tenant can easily do. But for the major repairs, plan on doing it in a timely fashion. It isn't fair to have your tenant wait 30 days to get heat in the winter. The landlord should keep a list of repair people if they can't do the repairs themselves. If the landlord can't repair something, other people's services need to be readily available. Of course, whatever the landlord can do himself will save a great deal of money. Therefore, if the landlord is handy and a "hands-on" type person, so much the better. Clarify to the tenant what you expect them to fix or repair. Tell them that they should fix a leaky faucet or running toilet. Put that statement in the lease. Otherwise, the landlord will be called at all times of the day and night.

SAMPLE MAINTENANCE CHECKLIST
1. Chimney: Inspect for deteriorated bricks, cracks, mortar, moisture, damage, rain caps. Clean regularly to prevent soot build-up
2. Roofs: Inspect for loose or missing shingles. Check flashing and downspouts.
3. Inspect gutters, downspouts and eaves.
4. Exterior walls: Check for settling, deterioration of building materials. Check for loose or rotted wood or boards.
5. Doors and Windows: Inspect the caulking and weather stripping. Replace any broken or cracked glass. Replace any rotted window trim.
6. Porches & Decks: Check for rot. Inspect the steps and railings for security and any rotted wood.
7. Garages: Test the door opener.
8. Trees & Shrubs: Cut back overhanging limbs. Keep shrubs trimmed.
9. Interior Heating: Check filters monthly and replace as needed. Inspect heating unit regularly and have regular maintenance. A/C: Check freon levels and have regular maintenance performed.
10. Attic: Inspect for mold or fungus. Watch for evidence of pests.
11. Plumbing: Check for leaks. Check faucets and toilets above and below.

WHO DOES WHAT?

LEAKY UPSTAIRS FAUCET DAMAGE

CHAPTER 12:
THE LANDLORD SHOULD PICK UP THE RENT IN PERSON

If the landlord doesn't find a way to get into their property, you will not be able to see how things are being maintained. Some excuses to get into the property are checking the furnace filters or checking anything that requires maintenance. You can also schedule monthly inspections. Specify in the lease that you will give the tenant 24 hours' notice to come in for an inspection. Whatever way is chosen to inspect the property, do it. Not inspecting your property is going to be a problem down the road. If the landlord goes in and sees damage, it can get fixed before it becomes a major issue. Also if the landlord sees extensive damage, the tenants are breaching the lease and you may want to file for eviction. Seeing the damages while the tenant is living there gives the landlord a chance to hold the tenants responsible for the damage. They will be more likely to pay for the damages if they are still living there. Once they are gone, they are not going to pay for anything. Even poor housekeeping should be noted. If the landlord sees that the place hasn't been cleaned and needs it badly, the landlord can give notice for it to be done. The landlord can come back and inspect again in a couple of weeks.

"IT'S NOT PERSONAL, IT'S BUSINESS"

If the landlord notices that the carpet hasn't been vacuumed in what looks like weeks and that the floors need mopping, it should be noted. The kitchen and bathroom are areas of the house that are often neglected. The landlord may feel embarrassed to point out bad housekeeping to the tenant. If it makes the landlord uncomfortable, put it in writing. Type up a list of what needs to be cleaned, repaired or improved. Send it to the tenant via email or regular mail. Just be sure to keep a copy for your records. Verbal conversations sometimes come across as personal, keep everything business-like by putting it in writing. The landlord must always remember that when it comes to running his rental business, IT'S NOT PERSONAL, IT'S BUSINESS. The landlord can be creative on ways to inspect the property. If you don't want to collect the rent in person, find other reasons. Go into the property and change the furnace filters, spray for insects, check the plumbing, whatever reason you can use. The landlord won't be sorry; it can save a lot of headache and expense to know what the tenant is doing to your property. If you don't get inside your property, you are going to find surprises when your tenant leaves!

PICK UP THE RENT!

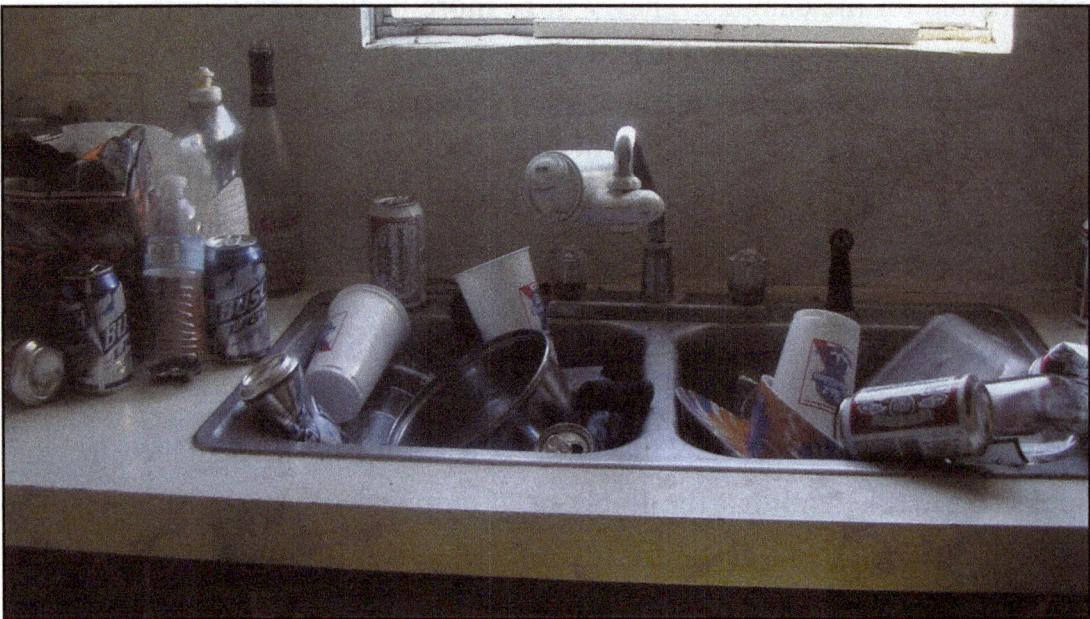

TENANTS WHO DON'T DO HOUSEKEEPING

TENANTS DON'T DO YARDWORK

SHEETROCK DAMAGE

TENANTS TRY TO COVER UP DAMAGE

CHAPTER 13:
THE LANDLORD MUST HAVE ADEQUATE NOTICE TO DO REPAIRS

Remember that your tenants may "freak out" when something breaks. This is especially the case with heating and air-conditioning. If they lose those, they will be upset. Can you fix it or do you need to call a specialist? You may want to check it yourself first and see if you can repair it. It may be as simple as a blown fuse or the a/c needs freon. But if you can't fix it, call someone. As a landlord, your tenants should not expect to call you in the middle of the night. Landlords are human. They can't expect you to get up at 2:00 in the morning in a snow storm to come and fix their heat. They have to be reasonable and give you adequate notice to fix it yourself or find someone else to fix it. State laws also dictate how much time you have to fix it. It could be up to 30 days. So don't feel like you have to jump and get right on it. You just have to be reasonable. If they have small children and the heat goes out, you want to fix it as soon as possible. But in most cases, it is not a matter of life or death. Even a roof leak can be lived with until the repair person comes out. The tenant can't expect miracles from you. The lease should specify how much notice they must give you and how long you have to respond. One property manager had students trying to call him at all hours. So finally when they called in early morning hours, he told them he could only respond if they met him at the police station because he felt threatened. Tenants can and will get hostile when things break down. They can become irrational and hostile. This is where you have to be diplomatic and calmly explain to them that you will fix it as soon as possible but not in the middle of the night. If you feel threatened by a tenant, you have the option to call the police.

THE TENANT WHO HATED BUGS

There was a tenant who felt she needed to call the landlord whenever she saw a bug inside the property. She evidently was afraid of bugs and transferred that to the landlord with numerous calls at all times. The landlord repeatedly told her to spray with bug killer when she wasn't going to be home. The advice was to spray inside and outside with bug spray. Finally, the calls continued and the landlord went to the property to inspect. There were tiny black specks of bugs from outside. The deck area hadn't been weeded and bugs were coming from that area. The tenant had removed all of the landlord's drapes because she thought bugs were inside of them. She had created a huge problem out of a small bug situation. This same tenant complained about the fridge not working. She claimed that the fridge door wouldn't close properly and that the defrost would come on. The landlord patiently went to the fridge and inspected. She had the fridge door so full of bottles that it was not level.

He fixed it by leveling it but she continued to call. The next time he went there, he noticed water on the floor. Water was on the floor of the kitchen and was leaking onto the dining room floors where new hardwood had been installed. She hadn't noticed that the hardwood flooring was being damaged, she was only focused on the fridge. The landlord had to replace all the hardwood flooring. He also shut off the ice maker so that it wouldn't leak. Was that enough to fix the problem? Absolutely not! She called and called until finally he went out and bought a new fridge and had it delivered. However, he refused to allow her to hook up the ice-maker. There was no way he was going to take the chance of ruining the new flooring again. The landlord has to be reasonable and objective in handling repairs. The tenant also needs to be reasonable and objective when demanding that something be fixed.

I NEED MY LIGHT BULB CHANGED

Jim had lived in the rental house for over 16 years. He paid his rent on time and was never behind. He had a full-time steady job as a chef at a well-known restaurant. He had been a widower since he moved into the property. Basically, Jim and the landlord got along pretty well. The landlord figured that since Jim lived alone that he must be keeping up with the house. When the landlord went to pick up the rent, the house appeared to be ok. The landlord wouldn't go so far as to say that the house was super clean but it wasn't destroyed either. Overall, the house was being kept up on the inside and Jim kept the exterior in fair shape. He cut the grass pretty regularly although he occasionally missed a week. Jim was a pretty good tenant, except that he couldn't repair a single thing. Jim was not a handyman by any standards. He knew nothing about fixing leaky faucets or running toilets. His lease stated that he was responsible to do these minor repairs. In his 16 years at the property, he was lucky in the sense that not many things needed repair. If they did, he didn't say anything about it. But occasionally, Jim would call the landlord to fix things. Normally, the landlord would have told the tenant to fix it themselves but the landlord knew that Jim couldn't fix anything. One day, Jim called the landlord to tell him that his living room lights weren't working. He thought the electrical breakers were blown. The landlord immediately went to the breaker box and checked all the fuses. Everything seemed to be in order. The fuses were all good.

"I can't find a blown fuse. Everything is fine," he told Jim.

"Well, my overhead lights won't turn on. I have tried them over and over," Jim explained.

"Well, let me check the light fixture, maybe it needs replacing," the landlord said, getting his ladder.

The landlord got up on the ladder and loosened the light fixture to check the wires. Everything seemed fine as he examined the light fixture. He tightened the light bulbs in the fixture before he got down from the ladder.

"I don't see anything wrong" he told Jim. He walked over to the light switch to try the lights and nothing happened.

"How about giving me a new light bulb?" he instructed Jim. The landlord replaced a bulb and then tried the light. The lights immediately came on.

"It was the light bulb that needed replacing. You mean to tell me that you didn't check the bulbs?" he asked Jim in amazement.

"Sorry, I didn't even think about checking the bulbs," Jim said with a red face.

"You have to get some handyman skills, Jim," the landlord said as he left in disbelief.

THE LANDLORD MUST HAVE NOTICE

MOUNTAIN CONDO

CHAPTER 14:
THE LANDLORD MUST HAVE WORKING CAPITAL TO DO REPAIRS

There will be damages at one time or another so be prepared. If the damages are extensive, the deposit will not cover them. Most deposits equal the monthly rent payment so if your rent payment is $1,000, the deposit is $1,000. If the damages are anything like the ones described in this book, $1,000 isn't going to cover the damages. The landlord will incur out of-pocket expenses. If the tenant has ruined the carpet, that is going to cost somewhere in the range of a couple thousand dollars. Painting a room may cost a couple hundred dollars but painting the entire house is going to be in the thousands. Replacing appliances will be in the thousands. What if the heating and cooling system need to be replaced? That could be anywhere from a couple thousand to ten thousand dollars. Plumbing issues? That could be anywhere from a couple hundred to thousands of dollars.

If the landlord has to hire people to do the work, the cost will rise tremendously. The only way that the landlord is going to save on the cost is if he can do the job himself. Hiring a plumber isn't going to be cheap for major repairs. There have been tenants who poured grease down the drain. That is a big problem. Grease should under no circumstances be poured down a drain. It will create a blockage in the plumbing pipes. The same goes for putting diapers and pads down the toilet. Tenants will do these types of things and not realize the type of damage that it causes. There was a situation where a tenant cleaned out the refrigerator and decided to put the thrown out food down the toilet. It created a major blockage in the plumbing pipes. That plumbing bill cost in the thousands of dollars. Who is responsible? Should the tenant pay due to their mistake? How will you get them to pay the bill? Some leases do include a statement about tenants putting things down the drain and/or toilet. It can state that the tenant is responsible for the damage caused by their negligence.

If the landlord can't fix it, be prepared for these expenses. Make sure that you record all of these expenses to be used as deductions on the property. When the landlord does their taxes, their income is not going to be anywhere near the amount of rent they collected. The expenses will be far more than the landlord expected.

YOU MUST HAVE CAPITAL

CARPET DAMAGE

FLOOR DAMAGE

DAMAGE TO KITCHEN CABINETS

DAMAGED KITCHEN SINK

WHO TOOK THE DISHWASHER?

DID I LEAVE MY FRIDGE?

WHO'S RESPONSIBLE FOR THE TRASH?

GARBAGE GETS LEFT

TENANTS ROLL OVER THE GAS TANK

TENANTS LOVE TO LEAVE TRASH

TENANTS TEAR OFF FRONT OF THE OVEN

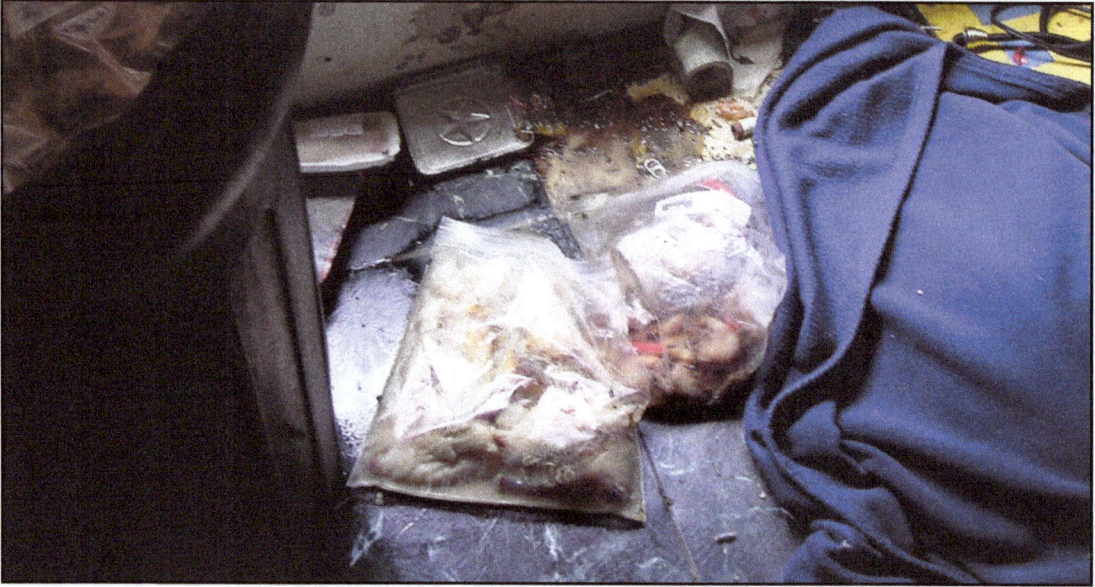

TENANTS LEAVE RAW MEAT

TENANTS LEAVE GARBAGE

CHAPTER 15:
THE LANDLORD SHOULD NEVER GIVE THEIR HOME ADDRESS OR HOME TELEPHONE

There is a very good reason for this rule. Think about it. Do you want tenants coming to your house? It's bad enough that they can call you but visit you? Remember that tenants can get hostile and you don't want a hostile tenant coming over. Keep things strictly on a business level, do not have any personal relationship with the tenant. Business is business and keep it that way. You are not renting to your friend; you are renting to a stranger.

THE TENANT WHO NEEDED TO GRILL HIS STEAK

One landlord rented a small mobile home to a single guy. The guy worked nearby and needed a small place to stay. He worked regular daytime hours and would come home from work and relax. On the weekends, he liked to drink beer and have friends over. There weren't any problems. The tenant appeared to be ok. After all, it was just one guy by himself. One summer day, the tenant's fridge went out. It just stopped cooling on the inside. It was a small fridge with a small amount of groceries in it. But the man didn't see it that way. He was very upset when the fridge stopped cooling. He had one steak in the freezer that he planned on cooking that night. He immediately called the landlord. His call went straight to voicemail. He left an angry message. He waited a short while for the landlord to return the call.

When there was not a response, he went to the landlord's office. No one was there when he arrived. He angrily went back home and repeatedly called the landlord. He still didn't get a response. The man got back in his car and went to the landlord's office. No one was there. The people who had a business next door to the tenant were there. The man went over to their business.

"Where in the hell is Mr. Smith?" he asked.

"I think he is in meetings all day today. He left his office early this morning," they told him.

"Well, what about his wife? Where do they live?" the tenant asked. The men gave the tenant the landlord's address. It never occurred to them that he would cause trouble. The man jumped in his car and sped off to the landlord's address. It didn't take him long to drive there. He pulled into the drive-way and marched up to the front door. He rang the doorbell several times. The landlord's wife answered the door. She saw a short man with a cigarette dangling from his mouth. The man was waving his hand all around.

"I'm Joe and I rent the mobile home from your husband," he angrily began.

"You need to go to our business office," she told him.

"Lady, I already been there. I have been trying to get ahold of your husband all morning. My fridge is broke. I got a steak that I want to cook and it is going to spoil I need that fridge fixed immediately," he explained blowing cigarette smoke in her face.

"You will have to wait until he returns your call. I can't help you," she said shutting the door. The man raced to his car and sped off.

Things didn't get too ugly but they could have. The tenant could have hurt someone or the police could have been called. The tenant was out of control over one steak. Imagine if it had been a fridge full of food. Give the tenant your business number and cell phone number. Do not give your home address or telephone number. Keep the home phone number out of the telephone directory. Some tenants believe that since they pay you money, you owe them.

DON'T GIVE YOUR ADDRESS

TENANT'S GRILL

CHAPTER 16:
THE UTILITIES SHOULD BE IN THE TENANT'S NAME PRIOR TO MOVE-IN

Do you want to get stuck paying the tenant's utilities? It happens all the time. The landlord may not insist or forget to switch the utilities over to the tenant's name. The tenant may claim that they don't have the money to pay the landlord back for the utilities. So the landlord is stuck with the bills. This could amount to huge heating and cooling bills. No tenant should be moving in before those utilities are switched. In addition, the landlord should contact the utility company and inform them that the power should never be shut off. When a tenant moves, the utility should go back in the landlord's name. This way there won't be a lapse in power. The power bill adds up fast. If your tenant moves in during the winter months, their monthly heat bill will be high. The same goes for the summer months when air-conditioning is used. This could be a tremendous bill for the landlord to pay. Once it gets too high, the chances of the tenant catching up with it are low.

Also, don't let the utilities get cut off. If the tenant fails to pay them, they will be shut off. If they can't pay utilities, they can't pay rent. So the landlord will be filing for eviction. Not having power means that you will have a mess from the fridge, damage with pipes if it is wintertime and all kinds of damage caused by not having power. The landlord can have an agreement with the utility company that if for any reason, the tenant doesn't pay, call the landlord and they will put the utilities back in their name. Of course, you will have to evict the tenants when you do that.

The tenant will be responsible for their utility bills and the landlord will be responsible only when they are put back in their name. It is better for the landlord to put them in their name rather than have damage.

The landlord had a property that was about an hour away from where he lived. The house and land were in a private rural setting. It wasn't a convenient location to pick up the rent each month. The landlord tried to rent the house with an option to purchase. It didn't take long to find a person who wanted to lease to own. Not only did they want to lease to own, they were willing to purchase the house on a land contract with the landlord. They would pay a down payment and the monthly payments would go towards the purchase price. It would all be written up legally through an attorney. This was an advantageous way of financing for the landlord and the tenant. On a land contract purchase, the landlord will get a monthly payment, a down payment and interest. The landlord is acting as the bank. If the tenant fails to make a payment, the landlord regains possession of the house. For the tenant, it gives them a chance to own a house without having to qualify for a bank mortgage. As long as they have a down payment, they make the rent payment just like a mortgage payment. It can work really well for both parties involved. The disadvantage is that the landlord gets the property back if the tenant misses a payment. The disadvantage for the tenant is that they can easily lose the property by missing a payment. All the terms and conditions were written up in a legal contract.

THE TENANT WHO PROVIDED THEIR OWN HEAT

The landlord had leased to a single man who traveled a lot for his job. As in the previous story, this tenant leased for several months before he approached the landlord about purchasing the house. The tenant didn't have good credit but he did have a down payment and a good job.

"I don't see any point in renting if I can own this house. Would you be willing to sell it to me without me going to the bank?" he asked the landlord.

"I have financed homes before on land contract. I am willing to sell it to you with a good enough down payment," the landlord told him.

"I can give you $5,000 cash for a down payment. My job is doing well and I have saved some money," the tenant explained.

"You've got a deal," the landlord said shaking the man's hand.

The landlord typed up a legal agreement for the man to purchase his house. He had sold houses before that he financed. If the man didn't pay the entire purchase price according to the agreement, the landlord would get the house back. This type of arrangement seemed acceptable for this tenant. The way it works is that the buyer pays a down payment, makes monthly payments, pays an interest amount set by the seller and agrees to so many years to pay the mortgage on the house. The purchase agreement is filed at the courthouse in the county where the property is located. An attorney can draw up the agreement or the landlord can do it if he is experienced enough. In this case, the landlord typed up the agreement, had the tenant sign it, got his down payment and then filed it in the county's records.

Everything went fine for about a year. The tenant made his monthly payments and then stopped. The tenant didn't answer the landlord's phone calls or eventually the landlord's letters. So the landlord traveled to the property to see what had happened. When he arrived, no one was at the house. He looked around and saw no evidence of anyone living there. He peeked inside the windows and there wasn't any furniture or sign of people living in the house. He went to the front door and it was unlocked. He slowly went inside and found a big mess. The house was vacant other than garbage and debris thrown around. He smelled kerosene and noticed a kerosene heater in the bedroom. The tenant had been burning kerosene inside the house which is very dangerous. He looked up and saw huge black soot marks on the ceiling. Evidently the tenant hadn't used the electric furnace heat. That could only mean one thing: he hadn't paid for the electric heat. The landlord left and called the electric company. They informed him that the electric was past due for 6 months and they had shut off the power. The landlord never saw or heard from the tenant again. The tenant lost the house and his $5,000 down payment.

UTILITIES IN TENANT'S NAME

FIRE PIT LEFT BY TENANTS

CHAPTER 17:
DO NOT ALLOW THE TENANT TO MAKE REPAIRS IN LIEU OF RENT

Occasionally you will have a tenant who comes up with the idea that he will do a repair instead of paying the rent. This may seem reasonable in the beginning. After all, if the tenant fixes something or repairs something, it saves the landlord time and money. Wrong! Most people are somewhat handy but are they true handymen? Usually the case is no. We all may be able to fix a leaky faucet or even repair a running toilet. But do most people have the skill to do a specialty job? Specialty work could include installing flooring, painting, installing tile, staining a deck, etc.

THE TILE INSTALLER

The tenant worked a regular job as a restaurant manager. He lived with his wife in the landlord's home for about a year. They paid the rent on time, they were quiet and created no problems for the landlord. When the tenant suggested taking up the carpet in the dining room of the house, the landlord listened.

"The carpet is old and worn. It would look a lot better to have tile in that room," the tenant suggested.

"I really don't want to spend the money on tile right now," the landlord replied.

"Oh no, I know how to do it. I was going to install it one weekend," the tenant explained.

"Have you ever installed tile?" the landlord asked cautiously.

"I did my mother's house last year," he said confidently.

"Ok, but just choose something neutral that matches the other flooring," the landlord instructed.

"I know where to get a really good deal on tile," the tenant said.

The tenant purchased tile from a friend who installed tile. He bought the left over tile from the guy's last job. The tile was big, 12 x 12 squares in a bright green color. It was not neutral tile as requested by the landlord. The tenant installed the tile that weekend. He didn't tell the landlord that he had only done a small section at his mother's house. So the man spent all weekend trying to figure out how to install the big tile squares. He was not sure about how much grout to use or the adhesive that goes underneath so he basically guessed at everything he did. He called his friend who was the tile installer but the friend was not available. In other words, the man "winged it." The finished tile job had loose tiles and crooked, thick grout lines. The bright green color was a big contrast to the adjoining flooring. It did not look good. The landlord came over to inspect the job and was rather shocked at what he saw.

"Why did you choose that color? I thought we agreed to use a neutral color," the landlord began.

"This was the tile that my friend had left over. Man, it was free," the guy said.

"Are you sure that you've installed tile before? The grout lines look awfully thick and crooked," the landlord said as he surveyed the damage.

"Look, this job was free. You didn't pay a thing. I think it looks pretty good," the guy said getting defensive.

The landlord walked away. There was no need to argue about it since the job was done. The guy wanted part of his rent discounted for doing the lousy tile job. What could the landlord do? The landlord shook his head. It was a mistake and he had to knock $300 off the guy's rent for the bad workmanship and horrible-looking tile. The landlord realized he would have to call a professional to fix the tile when the guy moved out. He wasn't going to fix it immediately since the guy did it. He could live with it for a time. Once the guy moves, the landlord will install carpet if need be. He shook his head for being so stupid!

Another landlord had a tenant who cleaned carpets for a living. The guy asked if he could clean the carpet every couple of months and deduct it from the rent. The landlord was pleased that the guy was cleaning the carpet and deducting $50.00 from the rent. But the landlord didn't go there and inspect the carpet each time. The guy was not cleaning the carpet at all, it was a lie. The carpet was filthy and dirty. When the landlord pointed that out to the guy, he became very angry. He insisted that he had been cleaning it. When he moved out, he decided to teach the landlord a little lesson. He took red kool-aid and poured it all on the off-white carpet in the living and dining rooms. The drink left huge red stains on the white carpet. It was impossible to remove the stains and the landlord had to take the carpet out and replace it.

NO WORK IN LIEU OF RENT

TILE WORK DONE BY A TENANT

CARPET WORK DONE BY A TENANT

CHAPTER 18:
IF THE RENT IS LATE, DON'T WAIT TOO LONG TO FILE FOR EVICTION

Know your state laws for eviction. In most states, the tenant is given a certain amount of days to respond to the eviction. The longer that the landlord waits, the more damage is done. If your tenant gets 2 or more months behind, it is going to be difficult to catch up. In the meantime, they can do more damage to your property.

Evicting a tenant requires that the landlord follow the process set out by their state law. If the term of the lease is ending, the landlord does not have to renew the lease. However, there must be a written lease with a specific term and the landlord must give written notice to the tenant that the lease will not be renewed and ask them to vacate within a reasonable time. If the tenant does not move after being asked to vacate (because the lease has ended or for other cause) a landlord may evict a tenant legally only by getting a court order. The landlord may not evict by changing locks or padlocking, turning off utilities and/or appliances, using threats or in any way other than through the court. The notice of eviction procedure in the state of North Carolina is covered by Chapter 42 of the general statutes passed by the state legislature. The landlord must comply with the rules in this statute for the eviction to be legal. Every landlord needs to check their state statutes.

SOME COMMON REASONS FOR EVICTION

- NON-PAYMENT OF RENT
- STAYING AFTER THE LEASE HAS ENDED
- BREACH OF THE LEASE
- CERTAIN CRIMINAL ACTIVITIES

The landlord must file a legal complaint with the court, stating grounds for the eviction. The complaint must be served on the tenant by the sheriff's office. There is a complaint form and a summons form. It will state when a court hearing will be usually within 10 days. Nothing in writing needs to be filed by the tenant.

The landlord or tenant may appeal the hearing decision within 10 days. The tenant may stay in the rental while the case is appealed if the tenant gets a "stay of execution" from the court. The tenant must pay the rent to the court. The landlord must not accept rent from the tenant during the eviction proceedings.

If the tenant loses final judgment in court, the landlord obtains a writ of possession from the Clerk of Court which the sheriff's office executes within 7 days. The sheriff will order the tenant to leave and padlock their belongings inside. The tenant will have 10 days to get their belongings. They must contact the landlord and arrange a time during regular business hours (or another time by agreement) to come and remove the property. If the tenant doesn't remove their belongings within those 10 days, the landlord may dispose of the property.

A tenant may NOT be evicted for:

1. Complaining or requesting that the landlord make repairs.
2. Complaining to the housing inspector or any government agency.

3. Any honest attempt by the tenant to enforce their rights under the lease.

4. Any honest attempt to organize, join or become involved with any group of people who are trying to help tenants.

Landlords cannot evict their tenants before the end of the lease without providing a written notice of eviction notifying them of the reason. For month-to-month tenants, landlords must provide at least 7 days' written notice of termination before the month ends. For a weekly tenant, landlords must provide 2 days' written notice before the beginning of the next week. North Carolina law doesn't require landlords to provide their tenants with an opportunity to cure an illegal lease violation such as illegal drug activities in their rental properties.

In summary, the landlord who wants to do an eviction must do the following:

1. Provide notice to the tenant

2. The landlord must obtain court forms to do a summary ejectment as well as the court summons delivered by the county sheriff.

3. The landlord must have a valid reason (non-payment of rent, staying after the lease is finished, or a breach of the lease)

4. After the eviction proceedings, the tenant has 10 days to appeal the eviction. Following the 10 day appeal period, if a tenant refuses to leave and hasn't filed appeal, the property will be padlocked by the sheriff. The landlord must file a writ of possession and the tenant has an additional 7 days to leave.

Check your state laws for eviction. In any event, it is time consuming and doesn't happen quickly. So the longer the landlord delays the legal process, the more time is wasted. Remember that you will probably have a lot of damage and repair work to complete before you can rent it again.

THE TENANT WHO APPEALED THE EVICTION

John and his wife lived in the landlord's rental property for a couple of years. John worked and his wife worked inside the home. They had 2 teenagers who went to the high school nearby. In the beginning, they always paid their rent on time. Eventually, the rent began to be late. It was starting to be a regular occurrence for them to be late. The landlord went to try and pick up the rent one day. The front yard was full of trash and debris. Trash was supposed to be picked up every week if the tenants rolled out their container to the curb.

"Why is your trash in the yard? It needs to be rolled out to the curb," the landlord told them.

"We've just been so busy lately," John replied.

"Well, your wife is home during the day. Can't she take it out and clean up the yard?" the landlord asked.

"No wife of mine is going to do yard work. That's my job," John said angrily.

"Well, your job keeps you pretty busy. You don't have much extra time," the landlord said.

"I'll get to it. She is not going to do it. That's my job," he angrily continued.

Weeks went by and the yard was still a mess. The rent was behind as usual. The landlord went back to the property.

"I can't have the yard looking like this and your rent is late again," the landlord told them.

"We have just had my wife's father move in with us. She is having to care for him. He's elderly and needs assistance. We'll get things caught up with the rent. We'll have his social security checks," John explained.

The landlord hesitated before he spoke. It was good that they would have extra income and he understood that the wife needed to help with her father. But they had moved him in without permission. The lease stated that they couldn't move new people in without approval. It was a judgment call for the landlord. He decided that it was ok for the father to live there. After all, he needed care and it would help pay their rent.

"You moved him in without letting me know. But I'm going to let it slide because he's elderly and will help with your rent," the landlord agreed. The rent was paid that day. But things didn't change as time went by. The rent continued to be late and then finally it got two months behind before the landlord took action. He sent the tenants their written notice to leave. He then went and filed the court papers and court summons for eviction. Of course, the tenants weren't happy about it. The landlord didn't understand why they weren't paying the rent when they now had extra income. All he knew is that they owed 2 months' rent.

The court day came and the tenants showed up. They didn't offer much in the way of why they hadn't paid their rent. They simply said that they had gotten behind on their bills and couldn't pay the rent. The judge listened and then made a judgment for the eviction.

Well, the landlord had done evictions before. He had done them many times in all his years of experience. But something new came up. The law in his state provided for the tenant to appeal the eviction. The tenant had 10 days to appeal it. These tenants did appeal the eviction based on the fact that the father lives with them. They claimed that he couldn't be moved right then. The landlord was flabbergasted. After all, the father was not part of the lease. He should never have allowed him to stay. They were using that as their reason to appeal. The appeal was granted and they were allowed to stay the rest of the lease term. The rent had to be paid to the court directly. They could not pay the landlord. If they paid the court late, they would be automatically evicted. The good part for the landlord was that they rent was to be paid to the court and couldn't be late. The checks were to be mailed to him from the court. The bad part was that this gave the tenants plenty of time to do more damage. Getting the rent wouldn't cover the damages.

The tenants stayed the duration of the lease. They paid all the months' rent on time to the court. What the court didn't understand was what the landlord often finds when the tenants leave. The property was destroyed worse than any other property that the landlord has ever owned. They had punched holes in the walls, holes in the floors, entirely ruined the carpet, cut the heating/ac lines and removed the plumbing for the appliances. The landlord took 5 trailers full of trash to the local dump. The damages exceeded $5,000. He knew he could take photos and file a complaint against them. But he also knew that they didn't have money to pay.

He would only get a judgment to be applied to his taxes. He wouldn't get a penny from these tenants. The tenants had also stolen building materials from a locked storage building on the property. So they had committed theft as well. But what could he do? Spend time in court or just count his losses? It's another judgment call that a landlord must make.

EVICTION STEPS:
1. File court papers in your county and pay the fees.
2. The tenant will be served the papers by the sheriff.
3. A court hearing will take place within two weeks.
4. If the landlord is granted the eviction, the tenant has ten days to leave or appeal the eviction.
5. If the tenant doesn't leave within the ten days, the landlord must file for a writ of possession to gain back their property. The landlord pays fees.
6. The sheriff delivers the writ of possession to the tenant within seven days following the filing. The sheriff comes out

the seventh day and has the landlord lock up the property and the tenant cannot come back in.

8. The tenant has 10 days to get any possessions left on the property. The tenant must pay storage fees to the landlord for keeping the possessions.

9. If the tenant files an appeal to the eviction, the court may grant it. If the court grants it, the tenant must pay the rent directly to the court. The court mails it to the landlord. If the tenant is even one day late, the appeal is terminated and the tenant has to move.

KNOW YOUR STATE'S LAWS

DID I LEAVE MY MATTRESS?

CHAPTER 19:
KEEP ALL DOCUMENTS AND PHOTOS FOR COURT

As you have read, you need to keep documents for any court hearings. Your photos and receipts will prove your case. Without them, you don't have a case. Keep your records accurate and organized for all situations that may arise. You have already seen how valuable records and photos are for the court system. The main things that you need for court are accurate payment records, notes, notices and photos.

You will also need to have accurate records for your tax returns. The IRS isn't going to take your word for your expenses and losses. The average person is thinking that the landlord charges $1,000 per month rent or he earns $12,000 per year. Wrong! Think about it.

EXPENSES

1. Property taxes
2. Insurance on the property
3. Any maintenance service such as the lawn
4. Regular maintenance or unexpected maintenance
5. Damages that have occurred to the property.
6. Court and attorney fees if the tenant doesn't pay them.

These are all deductions that have to be applied towards your earnings. By the time the landlord deducts these expenses, the earnings have dropped significantly. If a major maintenance issue arises, that is a huge loss (roof replacement, appliance replacement, heating/ac replacement, etc.) You have to keep accurate records on these deductions and losses. When the tenant pays, give them a receipt and keep it in your records. Note any late fees in your records. Note when you make inspections and when you do maintenance. Your accurate records will save you both time and money. Remember that the landlord is only going to profit a percentage of the rental money. For example if the tenant pays $1,000 per month or $12,000 per year, the landlord can expect to make a profit of around 60% or $7,200 after all of his expenses. That is provided that a major expense doesn't occur.

PHOTOS AND DOCUMENTS!

TENANT TAKES APPLIANCES

CHAPTER 20:
BE PRESENT WHEN THE TENANT MOVES OUT OF THE PROPERTY

This is a big rule that shouldn't be ignored. This one can really cost the landlord time and money. Remember that if the landlord isn't present, they can't see what the tenant leaves behind or what damage they do. Remember the young men who had the party the night before they left? Others can do the same or worse. This chapter could probably have a thousand stories. This is when you better have some working capital. Deposits won't cover these kinds of damages.

THE TENANT WHO LEFT THE LANDLORD A PRESENT

A family with three children lived in the landlord's mobile home on the lake. The peaceful lake setting was beautiful. The mobile home was modest but the surroundings were incredible. It was a private setting with a long, winding driveway. There weren't any neighbors nearby so the tenants could pretty much do as they pleased. Most people would appreciate such a nice setting that is so tranquil. But when someone gets behind in their rent, their attitude changes. All of a sudden, the landlord is the enemy. The home was located about an hour away from the landlord. The tenants mailed their rent check each month. In the beginning, they paid it on time. Eventually, the payments began to be late. Before long, the rent was going on 3 months past due. The landlord called them over and over. He never got an answer. He got a message that their phone was disconnected. He had no choice but to drive there in person. He had a conflict in schedule and decided to send his wife and son. They drove there on a late afternoon during the week.

They drove up the long driveway that was heavily wooded. At the top of the elevation was the mobile home. Immediately, they sensed that something was wrong. The porch railings were laying on the ground where they had been knocked off. The roof to the well house was off and laying on the ground. All the curtains were gone and you could see through the windows. Garbage was thrown everywhere around the house in the front and back yards. They got out of the car and looked at the outside damage. It was obvious that the family had moved. They weren't prepared for what they would find when they opened the front door. Right dead center of the living room was a bloody deer head. The stench was unbearable. The man had shot a deer and then purposely left its head in the home. They ran from the house and called the sheriff. The sheriff arrived within minutes.

"This is a rental home that we own. The people have left it without paying the rent. They have totally destroyed it. There is a deer head in the living room," they explained. The sheriff walked up to the front door and started to go in. He immediately turned around and ran out holding a handkerchief over his nose.

"Ma'am, don't go in there. That is not fit for humans. I forbid anyone to go in," he said holding the handkerchief to his nose.

"Sir, we have to go in. We own it, we can't just leave it," she told him.

"No ma'am, it's not habitable. You need to just burn it down. Forget about it," he said.

"Burn it down? We can't do that. It's a piece of property" she said.

"You do what you have to do. But I say it's destroyed and forget it," he said slightly gagging. He went to his car to write the report.

He gave them a police report and left. He wrote that the property was destroyed. But the landlord knew that though it was a total mess, it could be fixed. This guy didn't understand the rental business. It looked bad but this is how it goes in this business. Good, bad and ugly. He would get people to go in with masks and plastic clothes to clean it up. The landlord knew that you can't just abandon a property. Unless it is burned down, it is fixable. Obviously, the sheriff hadn't ever been a landlord. Landlords are used to seeing all kinds of horrible things.

BE PRESENT ON MOVE-OUT DAY!

TRASH LEFT BY TENANT

I DON'T DO DISHES

TRASHED GAZEBO

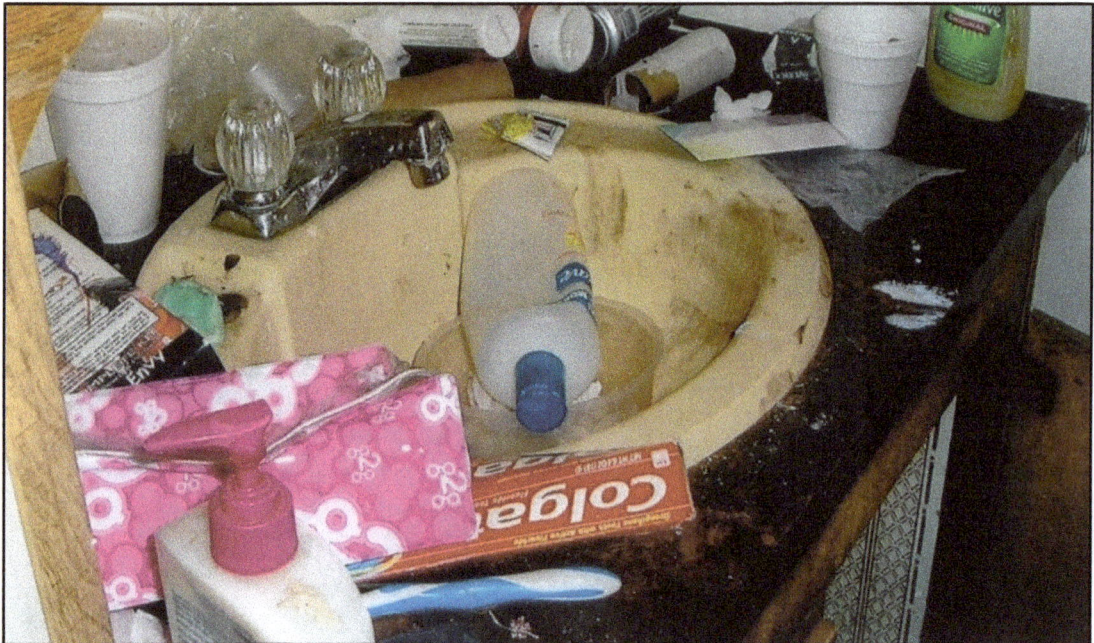

I FORGOT MY TOILETRIES

THE TENANT LEAVES A TRAMPOLINE

CHAPTER 21:
TAKE BEFORE AND AFTER PHOTOS

"A picture tells a thousand words" is a very accurate quote. This rule cannot be stated enough. Photos are going to be your only source of evidence in a dispute. If you have photos of your property when the tenant moves in, it will show exactly what the property looked like. The afterwards photos will show exactly what if any damages the tenant did to the property. This will serve you well when it comes to the tenant requesting their deposit back. DO NOT GIVE DEPOSITS BACK FOR AT LEAST 30 DAYS! This will give you adequate time to do a full inspection. If you give the deposit back without a full inspection, you may come across more damage than you expected. One example is that a tenant stole the actual well pump for a rural property. The landlord never knew that the pump was stolen until he went to turn the water on. No water! He went outside and, lo and behold, there was no pump to pump the water from the well. Tenants also like to steal the appliances. The landlord might go in and do an inspection when the tenants are moving and think that's it. But when they go back, the appliances are gone. Get the key to the property when the tenant moves and then go back for the final inspection. Their deposit may cover the damages or it may not be near enough to cover the damages.

A PHOTO IS WORTH A THOUSAND WORDS

A landlord filed eviction against a tenant for non-payment of rent and damages. The tenant was 2 months behind on the rent. The landlord had followed the procedure for his state. The court documents had been filed and the sheriff had delivered a court summons to the tenant. The tenant was not required to show up. If the tenant wished to dispute the landlord's claim, they needed to show up. The tenants chose to make the court appearance.

"Sir, what claim do you have against the tenants?" the judge asked the landlord.

"Your honor, the defendants owe me rent for 2 months' time and they have done extensive damage to my property," the landlord replied.

"Is that true?" the judge asked the tenants.

"Your honor, we do owe 2 months' rent because I got my hours cut at work. But we didn't do damage to his property," the tenant said.

"What kind of damages do you claim they have done, sir?" the judge asked the landlord. With that question, the landlord pulled out a stack of photos. He chose the top 4 photos.

"I would like to show you these photos, your honor," he said handing the photos to the bailiff. The judge took the photos and made a face as she looked at them. She put the photos down.

"I have heard cases for many years. In all that time, I have never seen photos like these. These are the most disgusting, vile photos. There are cat feces overflowing a litter box for at least a month. Did you do this?" she asked the tenant holding up the photo. Yes, your honor, that is from our cat," the tenant truthfully replied.

"Judgment for the plaintiff in the amount of $5,000," the judge stated firmly.

That was it. The case was closed and was in favor of the landlord. It was a simple, classic case where the photos won the case. The landlord breathed a sigh of relief, thankful that he took the photos. The hearing took less than 5 minutes with no speaking or arguing. The photos said it all.

BEFORE

AFTER

DIRTY TOILET IN TRASHED BATHROOM

TEENAGER'S BEDROOM

TEENAGER'S BATHROOM

MY KIDS DON'T CLEAN THEIR BEDROOMS

CHAPTER 22:
DEPOSITS SHOULD NEVER BE USED FOR RENT PAYMENTS

If the deposit is used for the last month's rent, what money can be used for damages? Deposits are strictly for damages and repairs. Some tenants request to use the deposit for rent if they don't have the money for the last month's rent. That is simply not going to work. Unless their property is spectacularly clean, there will be deductions made from the deposit. Most tenants don't get back the full deposit because the wear and tear on the property is beyond normal. Whether it be from their pets or heavy use, there may be damages from the best tenant. There may also be things that need repair. Maybe they didn't tell you about the stove burner that stopped working, the ceiling fan that has broken blades, the ice maker that stopped working and other items. It may not be their fault but they didn't tell you and you will need to fix or replace it.

A lot of tenants find that their move ends up being more of a hassle than they realized. They now realize when moving time comes, not only do they have to pack up and clean where they are living, they have to unpack and clean where they are going. It is a lot of work and maybe they didn't plan on it. So the new house usually gets first priority since they are going to be living there. Time runs out and they simply don't have time to clean the property like they should. They may end up leaving some furniture that they didn't have time to move. They may not clean the kitchen or bathrooms. Maybe they don't have time to run the vacuum over the carpet and mop the floors.

They may even leave their trash because they didn't take the time to take it to the garbage containers.

If the landlord has to take your bags of trash and move your furniture out, the tenant is going to get charged for it. The landlord didn't give the property to the tenant in that condition. When they moved in, there wasn't trash all over and furniture in the rooms. The property is expected to look the same as when the tenant moved in. The only thing that is normal wear and tear may be that some wall painting is needed and the carpet needs some cleaning. That is regular maintenance. But if the tenant's kids have colored all over the walls with crayons and markers, that is beyond normal wear and tear. The landlord has to completely repaint the entire house. If the tenant wants their deposit back, they need to make sure that everything is moved out with nothing left behind. (including pets) Nothing is left in the front and back yards including swing sets.

TENANT MOVE OUT LIST:

1. Nothing inside or outside (unless landlord approves leaving something)
2. No trash left anywhere.
3. Carpet vacuumed and clean
4. Floors swept and mopped
5. Kitchen appliances all cleaned (stove, fridge, dishwasher)
6. Kitchen cabinets cleaned inside and outside
7. Bathrooms cleaned (floors, tub, shower, sinks, toilet)
8. No evidence of pets left behind
9. Nothing broken that should have been reported to the landlord.
10. Nothing stolen (blinds, drapes, etc.)

If the tenant does this simple check list, there shouldn't be any problems with getting their Deposit back. If the tenant has completed this checklist, there should be no reason why the landlord can't do a final inspection with you.

NO RENT PAID FROM DEPOSIT

NO INSPECTION DONE

CHAPTER 23:
MAKE SURE YOU HAVE INSURANCE ON THE PROPERTY

People naturally purchase insurance on their residence and/or business. It is crucial that the landlord also purchases insurance on their rental properties. You want to make sure that you have insurance against fire, loss, theft and liability. Your tenants can do a lot of damage to your property including a fire. Remember the young men who almost burned down the house with burning furniture. Also a lot of tenants enjoy their bonfires. It is strongly suggested that you prohibit outdoor fireplaces or bonfires. They are popular in country, rural settings but why take the risk? Even allowing tenants to have fire pits or outdoor fireplaces is questionable. Tenants who live above other tenants in a condo or apartment-type structure should not be allowed to have any type of fire or grill on their patio or deck. All these requirements should be spelled out in the lease.

If theft occurs on the property, the landlord's insurance would cover the exterior and interior structure. It would not cover the renter's property or belongings. If your tenant desires to have renter's insurance, it is strongly recommended. They can purchase renter's insurance at a fairly low cost. There are many factors to consider when purchasing property insurance. Do you have enough coverage if the structure burned down? Would it cover total replacement?

If you own any mobile homes, that insurance is covered differently. Some companies don't cover older mobile homes and the landlord has to cover them with an extension clause on his personal residence insurance or purchase insurance from their state if they offer it.

The insurance on mobile homes is usually minimal. It will probably cover just fire or some other natural disaster. Check with several insurance companies to see what is offered in your state. But get it! Insurance on condos or townhouses can be tricky. If you have property that joins another structure such as a condo, different rules apply. Your policy may cover the interior for damages and the homeowner's policy may cover the exterior. The homeowner's may cover some of the interior damage too. You need to make sure that these items are clarified before you purchase the insurance.

IT WASN'T MY FAULT, I WASN'T THERE

One landlord owned a property that was a condo. The condo was a lower unit with a unit above it and a unit beside it. The landlord didn't have it rented and he didn't live nearby. He could only rely on the management to occasionally check on it. Not only was his unit vacant, the unit above was also vacant since it was for sale. The owner of the upper unit had left the area and placed it for sale. That owner had turned the power off but they didn't turn the water off. Big problem for the lower unit. A pipe burst in the upper unit. The pipe was in the ceiling of the lower unit. Water gushed out heavily. The water was so heavy that it ran out the bottom of the front door and the rear patio door. A passer-by noticed the water gushing out the patio doors. The person called 911. The police arrived to see the place totally flooded. They immediately called the management company for someone to come out with a key. The management arrived to open up the place. It was a total disaster. The place had flooded in minutes. The ceiling had collapsed, knocking down things on the ground. Water poured over every surface of the condo including all the furniture. The landlord was notified by telephone. He lived 2 hours away. He was at the mercy of the management company. He was not there to figure out what to do and had to trust them to handle the situation. They called a company to come and dry the place out. That company called the landlord and told him that he would need at least 5 days for the place to dry out. They ran special industrial sized machines to soak up all the moisture. The landlord was helpless until that process was completed. He had to travel the 2 hours to find workers to repair the place. That was time consuming and costly.

The landlord reported the flood to his insurance company. He was specific in telling them that it was from the unit above him and that their water line burst. He had nothing to do with the problem. Not so fast! That's not how the insurance company sees it. In his state, it was no fault insurance. Just because the flood came from the owner above, were they negligent? In his state, the homeowner has to be negligent in order to be responsible for the claim. It turned out the owner above had the same insurance company. To the shock of the landlord, the insurance adjuster told him that the claim would go on his policy. He couldn't prove that the owner above was negligent. So the owner above got off scott free and only had to pay the deductible to repair the broken water pipe. The landlord's insurance covered the interior damage. But the homeowner's policy covered the ceiling repair. So the cost was calculated with them involved too. The damage was around $30,000 and the homeowner's paid around $5,000 of the total. The owner upstairs paid $200.

To make matters worse, the landlord got the claim put on his policy which would always show up when he tries to purchase insurance in the future. It doesn't matter that it wasn't his fault, it would always show up as a claim. So he was penalized form something that he had nothing to do with. Every time the landlord goes to purchase insurance, he has to provide a letter of explanation from that claim. It was a bad scenario for the landlord but would have been much worse if he didn't have insurance.

Another situation is that of liability insurance. What if a tenant falls on your property due to a broken step? Will they file a claim against you? Maybe not you but they will file it against your insurance.

THE BROKEN LEG

The landlord knew a man who fixed lawnmowers. So he always took his mowers to this guy to be fixed. The man was in his 60s and was living on what little he made from fixing lawn mowers. One day, the man was telling the landlord how he needed to make some money. The landlord felt sorry for this man who needed extra money.

"I know it's not much work but I sure need help cutting grass on my property. I have a lot of acres to cut," the landlord told him.

"I'd be glad to help but I don't drive. If you pick me up, I'll help you," the man said. The next day, the landlord picked up the man from his home. He gave him instructions on what he needed done.

"I'm going to cut around the front of my property. If you would use the weed-eater in the rear, that would help," the landlord instructed. They gathered the weed-eater for the man to use.

"Just jump on the back of my tractor and hold on, I'll drive you to the rear," the landlord instructed. The man who was a little heavy-set jumped on the back of the landlord's tractor. It was an old tractor but sturdy. There was a place to ride on that was over the blades and had a bar to hold onto. The man held on and the landlord drove slowly.

"I'll be back in a couple hours," the landlord told the man when he dropped him off. The man began to work as the landlord left. The landlord worked on the front of the property for at least 2 hours when he noticed a truck pulling in. It was the man's brother.

"I just came to check on my brother and bring him a drink," the man in the truck explained. The landlord didn't pay any attention and continued to work. When he was finished, he hopped on his tractor to go and pick up the man.

"Well, let's call it a day, let's go," he told the man instructing him to get back on the back of the tractor. The man hopped on just like he did before. The landlord started down the path driving slowly. Suddenly he heard screaming. He brought the tractor to a stop and looked back. The man had fallen off the tractor and was lying on the ground screaming.

"I've fallen and I'm hurt," he yelled, grabbing at his leg.

"Can you get up? Let me help you," the landlord said trying to help.

"I can't get up. I feel like I might pass out. I'm diabetic, you know. I didn't eat all day," he said. The landlord smelled alcohol or liquor on the man's breath. Did the man's brother bring him beer or liquor? Did he fall because of drinking or being diabetic or both? Thoughts swirled in the landlord's mind. The man couldn't move and probably broke his leg. The landlord called an ambulance. He also called the man's wife. She arrived when the ambulance came.

"He's a diabetic and he probably didn't eat," she tried to explain to the medic.

"Well, it looks like he broke his leg," the medic said as he examined the leg.

They splinted the leg and the man left for the hospital. But that's not all. On the way to the hospital, the ambulance hit another car. The injured man had to wait while they called another ambulance. No one was hurt but he had to be transferred to another ambulance. The landlord went to the hospital a few hours later to check on the man. The man did have a broken leg. Since it was the weekend, he had to stay until Monday. Since he was older they wanted to make sure that he was ok by keeping him for medical tests.

"We don't have insurance since he doesn't work. Do you have homeowner's?" the man's wife asked the landlord. The landlord wasn't sure what to say. Since he felt badly that the man was hurt on his property, so he told her yes.

"I will check with my insurance company on Monday," he said.

Well, on Monday he called his insurance and it did cover liability for someone on the property. But the insurance company gave him a good scolding.

"You should never have let the man ride on the tractor," they scolded him.

"I was just trying to help him so that he didn't have to walk so far," he explained.

Dealing with the insurance wasn't easy. They called him back to have him give his side of the story.

He said that the truth was that the man did smell of liquor and that he is diabetic. Well, the insurance was happy with that. They had something to go on as far as having the man bear some of the responsibility. The man ended up having the insurance pay very little on a claim. He was a veteran and the veteran benefits ended up paying most of the claim. So the landlord didn't get a huge claim but he could have. The insurance was valuable to have. He was lucky that the man wasn't the type to go after him for more. At least he had insurance for back-up. So a landlord needs to make sure that they have insurance that covers all situations. Without it, you could lose a lot. It is protection that you can't do without.

> ## GET INSURANCE!

CHAPTER 24:
COMMERCIAL LEASES ARE DIFFERENT THAN RESIDENTIAL LEASES

Residential leases have been discussed. However, the landlord may also have commercial leases or property that is leased to businesses. The commercial lease requires a different type of lease. Generally, the lease is longer in length than a residential lease and the landlord needs even more protection. The landlord may have more valuable property with the commercial lease and it may be subject to more liability. Whenever a landlord leases to a tenant who has a business, there are going to be state, local and county ordinances and laws. For example, a business can only be in its designated zoning. A business that is industrial can't be in a retail location. Different zonings may include industrial, retail, commercial, multi-family, etc. Each of these zonings has specific requirements. If you rent to a retail business, you can be sure that certain criteria must be met. There will have to be adequate parking spaces, handicapped parking, handicapped bathrooms and other requirements. Each county has specific guidelines for different types of businesses. Your tenant may want you to accommodate these requirements. If you don't have parking for his type of business, you may not be able to rent it to him. The tenant may also want you to "outfit" his business (in other words, do improvements or remodeling that suits his type of business). If the tenant has a restaurant, the landlord may have to add special fire retardant walls, flooring and exhaust fans for the kitchen equipment. If the landlord makes all these changes to their property, the rent will have to be increased in order to get the return on their money spent outfitting the property. Another thing to consider is when the present tenant leaves. If that tenant had a specific type of business, the next tenant may have another type of business. Are you prepared to accommodate each time a tenant leaves? The tenant may leave you all kinds of built-in fixtures that the next tenant will not want.

THE FISH STORE

The landlord owned a rather old building in an area that was mixed use. The mixed use included residential and business mixed together. The building had been "grandfathered" in over the years. In other words, it had been a fish store for many years while the surrounding area had undergone change. The county allowed the building to be used as a fish store since it had been in existence for over 50 years. The landlord purchased the building and the tenant stayed doing business as a fish store. But the day came when he retired and no longer operated his business. The landlord had to work immediately to get another fish store into the building. If he let the building remain vacant, the "grandfather" clause no longer applied. The landlord did find another tenant who wanted to operate a fish store. The new tenant decided to make some changes to the building. He made those changes without the landlord's authorization or consent. Some of those changes required county inspection from the building department and health department. It was like opening up a can of worms in the sense that things escalated. The county then required rules and requirements for the new changes. The new tenant had a lot of unexpected expenses. Those expenses forced him to close his business. He couldn't make enough money to recoup his expenses. The landlord was then stuck with the building and its improvements that were for a fish store only. He had to continue on renting the building as a fish store. If he stops renting it as a fish store, he loses his "grandfather clause" and will be forced to do major improvements to the building to accommodate another type of business.

The commercial lease needs to be very solid in what it covers. Most commercial leases are longer in the length of the lease. The landlord cannot accept a short term lease in order to recoup their investment. If the landlord leases to a restaurant, you would expect to have at least a 5 year lease in order to recoup the investment. It all depends on how much the landlord invests in improvements or outfitting. The commercial lease is more detailed and will hold the tenant to the terms of the lease more strictly. It is a more costly investment and the landlord needs even more protection. The commercial lease may also involve people coming and going into the business. Therefore, more liability insurance would be needed. Your tenant also needs to cover insurance for the interior of the building as well as for their property.

COMMERCIAL LEASE SHOULD CONTAIN:
1. Longer lease term.
2. Specify type of business, permits, licenses, city ordinances required.
3. Zoning of the business.
4. Provisions for any outfitting of the business.
5. Provisions for the tenant's responsibility of their outfitting when they leave. Most landlords require that any attached fixtures must not be removed.
6. Any special provisions needed for the business.
7. A deposit that will cover damages.
8. Triple Net: Most commercial leases are triple net, meaning that the tenant does all maintenance to the property, pays the property taxes and pays for the insurance on the building and liability insurance. Landlord must be listed on the insurance policy.

UNDERSTAND A COMMERCIAL LEASE

RETAIL COMMERCIAL PROPERTY

RETAIL COMMERCIAL PROPERTY

BEAUTIFUL OLD ROCK BUILDING

CHAPTER 25:
CONSULT AN ATTORNEY IF NEEDED

This book has been told from one landlord's perspective. Through experience, the landlord has become familiar with their state's laws in regards to landlords and tenants. Every situation differs as well as state laws. First and foremost, the prospective landlord should be informed and knowledgeable about their state and county laws. You as a landlord want to abide by all required laws and regulations. The landlord is renting their property to make a profit. But in order to make a living from it, you have to know how to cut your losses and expenses. Hopefully, this book has given insight into how to do just that. If the landlord knows ahead of time what to do, the landlord will avoid that mistake at all costs. These recommendations, tips and advice are to give you some preparation for being a successful landlord. Without knowing what to expect, the landlord will make costly mistakes. Many beginning landlords have learned the hard way that mistakes cost lots of money. If the landlord is still uncertain about anything in regards to their rights and the tenant's rights, they should by all means contact an attorney. If the landlord isn't comfortable about going to a court hearing to evict a tenant, they may choose to hire an attorney to represent them. That is fine but remember that you are trying to cut expenses and losses. Once you understand the system of being a landlord, you will become more and more comfortable and able to handle all kinds of situations. If you know your state and county laws, keep accurate records, documents, photos and have a solid lease agreement, your risks are much less.

This book has advised you of potential situations that came up with tenants. Those situations were not positive in any way. That is not to say that you may not have some great tenants. If you have really good tenants, your job as a landlord will be much easier. There have been good tenants who really took pride in the landlord's property and treated it as if it were their own. They paid their rent on time, they did minor repairs, They seldom called the landlord and they even did some improvements to the property. That is the best situation for any landlord. But the fact is that if someone doesn't own the property, they may not take care of it like it was their own. They are paying someone rent and they expect that person to do all the repairs and maintenance. There are also people who are just not careful or clean. They don't respect their property and they don't care about cleaning it. Even if they owned a house, they may still not keep it clean. A landlord has to be realistic that not every person is clean and careful. A landlord may follow all the rules and laws for landlords but that landlord has to be prepared for all scenarios that may arise. As a landlord, I have seen it all and today nothing surprises me. It took years of experiences to get used to it but you finally come to accept it for what it is.

Hopefully, adding these recommendations and advice will make it even less risky for prospective landlords. Your chances of being a successful landlord should be much more improved. There are things that come up that even the most experienced landlord never expects. Knowing and following the guidelines set forth in this book should help the landlord overcome a lot of problems. The successful landlord can make a very good income if they learn and utilize these tips and advice. Once you learn these tips, you can move forward to avoid the problems and capitalize on making a good income. Rental property income can be a good source for a secondary income or even a primary income. The potential landlord needs to learn from experience and find what will make them successful with their rental properties.

USE AN ATTORNEY AS NEEDED

BUSINESS MAN TURNS INTO A LANDLORD

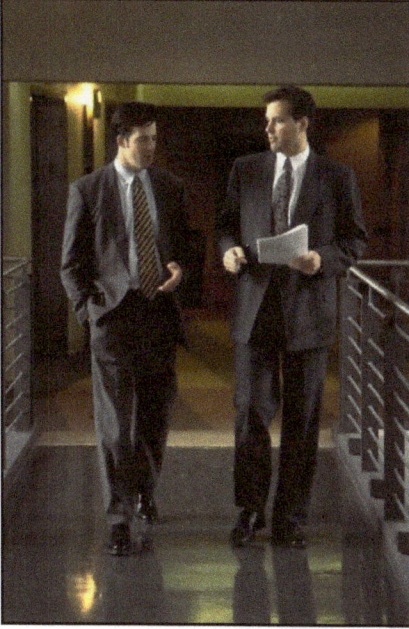

◄ BUSINESS MAN

LANDLORD ►

APPENDIX I:
SAMPLE RENTAL FORMS

COMPLAINT FOR MONEY OWED

COMPLAINT EJECTMENT

MAGISTRATE SUMMONS

WRIT OF POSSESSION

COMMERCIAL LEASE AGREEMENT

TENANT SELECTION CRITERIA CHECKLIST

LANDLORD'S NOTICE TO VACATE

FLOW CHART TO PURCHASE REAL ESTATE

PROPERY OWNER'S FINANCIAL FLOW CHART

RENTAL FLOW CHART -
10 STEPS FROM PRE-SCREENING TO LEASE SIGNING

REAL ESTATE ACQUISITION WORKSHEET

RENT RECEIPT

TIME FOR REPAIRS

TENANT MINOR MAINTENANCE LEASE

MOVE-OUT LETTER

PROPERTY RULES AND REGULATIONS

AMENDMENTS TO THE LEASE

File No.

**COMPLAINT
FOR MONEY OWED**

G.S. 7A-216, 7A-232

STATE OF NORTH CAROLINA

SAMPLE

_____ County

In The General Court Of Justice
District Court Division-Small Claims

Name And Address Of Plaintiff

County		Telephone No.

VERSUS

Name And Address Of Defendant 1   ☐ Individual ☐ Corporation

County		Telephone No.

Name And Address Of Defendant 2   ☐ Individual ☐ Corporation

County		Telephone No.

Name And Address Of Plaintiff's Attorney

1. The defendant is a resident of the county named above.
2. The defendant owes me the amount listed for the following reason:

Principal Amount Owed	► $
Interest Owed *(if any)*	► $
Total Amount Owed	► $

(check one below)

☐ On An Account *(attach a copy of the account)*

Date From Which Interest Due		Interest Rate

☐ For Goods Sold And Delivered Between

Beginning Date	Ending Date	Interest Rate

☐ For Money Lent

Date From Which Interest Due		Interest Rate

☐ On a Promissory Note *(attach copy)*

Date Of Note	Date From Which Interest Due	Interest Rate

☐ For a Worthless Check *(attach a copy of the check)*

☐ For conversion *(describe property)*

Other: *(specify)*

I demand to recover the total amount listed above, plus interest and reimbursement for court costs.

Date	Name Of Plaintiff Or Attorney (Type Or Print)	Signature Of Plaintiff Or Attorney

AOC-CVM-200, Rev. 2/12
© 2012 Administrative Office of the Courts

(Over)

INSTRUCTIONS TO PLAINTIFF OR DEFENDANT

SAMPLE

1. The PLAINTIFF must file a small claim action in the county where at least one of the defendants resides.

2. The PLAINTIFF cannot sue in small claims court for more than $5,000.00 excluding interest and costs.

3. The PLAINTIFF must show the complete name and address of the defendant to ensure service on the defendant. If there are two defendants and they reside at different addresses, the plaintiff must include both addresses. The plaintiff must determine if the defendant is a corporation and sue in the complete corporate name. If the business is not a corporation, the plaintiff must determine the owner's name and sue the owner.

4. The PLAINTIFF may serve the defendant(s) by mailing a copy of the summons and complaint by registered or certified mail, return receipt requested, addressed to the party to be served or by paying the costs to have the sheriff serve the summons and complaint. If certified or registered mail is used, the plaintiff must prepare and file a sworn statement with the Clerk of Superior Court proving service by certified mail and must attach to that statement the postal receipt showing that the letter was accepted.

5. The PLAINTIFF must pay advance court costs at the time of filing this Complaint. In the event that judgment is entered in favor of the plaintiff, court costs may be charged against the defendant.

6. The DEFENDANT may file a written answer, making defense to the claim, in the office of the Clerk of Superior Court. This answer should be accompanied by a copy for the plaintiff and be filed no later than the time set for trial. The filing of the answer DOES NOT relieve the defendant of the need to appear before the magistrate to assert the defendant's defense.

7. Whether or not an answer is filed, the PLAINTIFF must appear before the magistrate.

8. The PLAINTIFF or the DEFENDANT may appeal the magistrate's decision in this case. To appeal, notice must be given in open court when the judgment is rendered, or notice may be given in writing to the Clerk of Superior Court within ten (10) days after the judgment is rendered. If notice is given in writing, the appealing party must also serve written notice of appeal on all other parties. The appealing party must PAY to the Clerk of Superior Court the costs of court for appeal within twenty (20) days after the judgment is rendered.

9. This form is supplied in order to expedite the handling of small claims. It is designed to cover the most common claims.

10. **The Clerk or magistrate cannot advise you about your case or assist you in completing this form. If you have any questions, you should consult an attorney.**

AOC-CVM-200, Rev. 2/12
© 2012 Administrative Office of the Courts

153

STATE OF NORTH CAROLINA

SAMPLE

_____ County

In The General Court Of Justice
District Court Division-Small Claims

**COMPLAINT
IN SUMMARY EJECTMENT**

G.S. 7A-216, 7A-232; Ch. 42, Art. 3 and 7

Name And Address Of Plaintiff

County | Telephone No.

VERSUS

Name And Address Of Defendant 1   □ Individual   □ Corporation

County | Telephone No.

Name And Address Of Defendant 2   □ Individual   □ Corporation

County | Telephone No.

Name And Address Of Plaintiff's Attorney Or Agent

File No. ▲

1. The defendant is a resident of the county named above.
2. The defendant entered into possession of premises described below as a lessee of plaintiff.

Description Of Premises (Include Location)

□ Conventional
□ Public Housing
□ Section 8

Type Of Lease
□ Oral   □ Written

Rate Of Rent		Date Rent Due	Date Lease Ended
$	per □ Month □ Week		

3. □ The defendant failed to pay the rent due on the above date and the plaintiff made demand for the rent and waited the 10-day grace period before filing the complaint.

□ The lease period ended on the above date and the defendant is holding over after the end of the lease period.

□ The defendant breached the condition of the lease described below for which re-entry is specified.

□ Criminal activity or other activity has occurred in violation of G.S. 42-63 as specified below.

Description Of Breach/Criminal Activity (give names, dates, places and illegal activity)

4. The plaintiff has demanded possession of the premises from the defendant, who has refused to surrender it, and the plaintiff is entitled to immediate possession.
5. The defendant owes the plaintiff the following:

Description Of Any Property Damage

Amount Of Damage (If Known)	Amount Of Rent Past Due	Total Amount Due
$	$	▲ $

6. I demand to be put in possession of the premises and to recover the total amount listed above and daily rental until entry of judgment plus interest and reimbursement for court costs.

Date | Name Of Plaintiff/Attorney/Agent (Type Or Print) | Signature Of Plaintiff/Attorney/Agent

CERTIFICATION WHEN COMPLAINT SIGNED BY AGENT OF PLAINTIFF

I certify that I am an agent of the plaintiff and have actual knowledge of the facts alleged in this Complaint.

Date | Name Of Agent (Type Or Print) | Signature Of Agent

(Over)

AOC-CVM-201, Rev. 2/12
© 2012 Administrative Office of the Courts

154

INSTRUCTIONS TO PLAINTIFF OR DEFENDANT

1. The PLAINTIFF must file a small claim action in the county where at least one of the defendants resides.

2. The PLAINTIFF cannot sue in small claims court for more than $5,000.00 excluding interest and costs.

3. The PLAINTIFF must show the complete name and address of the defendant to ensure service on the defendant. If there are two defendants and they reside at different addresses, the plaintiff must include both addresses. The plaintiff must determine if the defendant is a corporation and sue in the complete corporate name. If the business is not a corporation, the plaintiff must determine the owner's name and sue the owner.

4. The PLAINTIFF may serve the defendant(s) by mailing a copy of the summons and complaint by registered or certified mail, return receipt requested, addressed to the party to be served or by paying the costs to have the sheriff serve the summons and complaint. If certified or registered mail is used, the plaintiff must prepare and file a sworn statement with the Clerk of Superior Court proving service by certified mail and must attach to that statement the postal receipt showing that the letter was accepted.

5. In filling out number 3 in the complaint, if the landlord is seeking to remove the tenant for failure to pay rent when there is no written lease, the first block should be checked. (Defendant failed to pay the rent due on the above date and the plaintiff made demand for the rent and waited the ten (10) day grace period before filing the complaint.) If the landlord is seeking to remove the tenant for failure to pay rent when there is a written lease with an automatic forfeiture clause, the third block should be checked. (The defendant breached the condition of the lease described below for which re-entry is specified.) And "failure to pay rent" should be placed in the space for description of the breach. If the landlord is seeking to evict tenant for violating some other condition in the lease, the third block should also be checked. If the landlord is claiming that the term of the lease has ended and the tenant refuses to leave, the second block should be checked. If the landlord is claiming that criminal activity occurred, the fourth block should be checked and the conduct must be described in space provided.

6. The PLAINTIFF must pay advance court costs at the time of filing this Complaint. In the event that judgment is rendered in favor of the plaintiff, court costs may be charged against the defendant.

7. The PLAINTIFF must appear before the magistrate to prove his/her claim.

8. The DEFENDANT may file a written answer, making defense to the claim, in the office of the Clerk of Superior Court. This answer should be accompanied by a copy for the plaintiff and be filed no later than the time set for trial. The filing of the answer DOES NOT relieve the defendant of the need to appear before the magistrate to assert the defendant's defense.

9. The PLAINTIFF or the DEFENDANT may appeal the magistrate's decision in this case. To appeal, notice must be given in open court when the judgment is entered, or notice may be given in writing to the Clerk of Superior Court within ten (10) days after the judgment is entered. If notice is given in writing, the appealing party must also serve written notice of appeal on all other parties. The appealing party must PAY to the Clerk of Superior Court the costs of court for appeal within twenty (20) days after the judgment is entered.

10. If the defendant appeals and wishes to remain on the premises the defendant must also post a stay of execution bond within ten (10) days after the judgment is entered.

11. This form is supplied in order to expedite the handling of small claims. It is designed to cover the most common claims.

12. **The Clerk or magistrate cannot advise you about your case or assist you in completing this form. If you have any questions, you should consult an attorney.**

SAMPLE

AOC-CVM-201, Side Two, Rev. 2/12
© 2012 Administrative Office of the Courts

STATE OF NORTH CAROLINA

SAMPLE

File No.

_____ County

In The General Court Of Justice
District Court Division - Small Claims

Plaintiff(s)

VERSUS

Defendant(s)

MAGISTRATE SUMMONS

☐ **ALIAS AND PLURIES SUMMONS (ASSESS FEE)**

G.S. 7A-217, -232; 1A-1, Rule 4

Date Original Summons Issued

Date(s) Subsequent Summons(es) Issued

TO:

Name And Address Of Defendant 1

TO:

Name And Address Of Defendant 2

A Small Claim Action Has Been Commenced Against You!

You are notified to appear before the magistrate at the specified date, time and location of trial listed below. You will have the opportunity at the trial to defend yourself against the claim stated in the attached complaint.

You may file a written answer, making defense to the claim, in the office of the Clerk of Superior Court at any time before the time set for trial. Whether or not you file an answer, the plaintiff must prove the claim before the magistrate.

If you fail to appear and defend against the proof offered, the magistrate may enter a judgment against you.

Date of Trial

Time Of Trial ☐ AM ☐ PM

Location Of Court

Name And Address Of Plaintiff Or Plaintiff's Attorney

Date Issued

Signature

☐ Deputy CSC   ☐ Assistant CSC   ☐ Clerk Of Superior Court

AOC-CVM-100, Rev. 6/11
© 2011 Administrative Office of the Courts

(Over)

ARE YOU SURE YOU WANT OT BE A LANDLORD?

RETURN OF SERVICE

I certify that this Summons and a copy of the complaint were received and served as follows:

DEFENDANT 1

Date Served	Time Served	Name Of Defendant
	☐ AM ☐ PM	

☐ By delivering to the defendant named above a copy of the summons and complaint.

☐ By leaving a copy of summons and complaint at the dwelling house or usual place of abode of the defendant named above with a person of suitable age and discretion then residing therein.

☐ As the defendant is a corporation, service was effected by delivering a copy of the summons and complaint to the person named below.

Name And Address Of Person With Whom Copy Left (If Corporation, Give Title Of Person Copy Left With)

☐ Other manner of service: (specify).

☐ Defendant WAS NOT served for the following reason:

DEFENDANT 2

Date Served	Time Served	Name Of Defendant
	☐ AM ☐ PM	

☐ By delivering to the defendant named above a copy of the summons and complaint.

☐ By leaving a copy of summons and complaint at the dwelling house or usual place of abode of the defendant named above with a person of suitable age and discretion then residing therein.

☐ As the defendant is a corporation, service was effected by delivering a copy of the summons and complaint to the person named below.

Name And Address Of Person With Whom Copy Left (If Corporation, Give Title Of Person Copy Left With)

☐ Other manner of service: (specify).

☐ Defendant WAS NOT served for the following reason:

FOR USE IN SUMMARY EJECTMENT CASES ONLY

☐ Service was made by mailing by first class mail a copy of the summons and complaint to the defendant(s) and by posting a copy of the summons and complaint at the following premises.

Date Served	Name(s) Of The Defendant(s) Served By Posting

Address Of Premises Where Posted

Service Fee	Signature Of Deputy Sheriff Making Return
$	
Date Received	Name Of Sheriff (Type Or Print)
Date Of Return	County Of Sheriff

AOC-CVM-100, Side Two, Rev. 6/11
© 2011 Administrative Office of the Courts

SAMPLE

157

STATE OF NORTH CAROLINA

SAMPLE

File No.

Film No.

_____ County

In The General Court Of Justice

Name And Address Of Plaintiff

WRIT OF POSSESSION
REAL PROPERTY

G.S. 1-313(4); 42-36.2

VERSUS

Name And Address Of Defendant 1

Name And Address Of Defendant 2

To The Sheriff Of_____ **County:**

A judgment in favor of the plaintiff was rendered in this case for the possession of the real property described below; and you are commanded to remove the defendant(s) from, and put the plaintiff in possession of those premises.

Description Of Property (include location)

Date Of Judgment

Date Writ Issued

Signature

☐ Deputy CSC   ☐ Assistant CSC   ☐ Clerk Of Superior Court

(Over)

AOC-CV-401, Rev. 11/99
© 1999 Administrative Office of the Courts

RETURN OF SERVICE

☐ 1. This Writ Of Possession was served as follows:

    ☐ a. By removing the defendant(s) from the premises and putting the plaintiff in possession after giving notice of removal to the defendant(s) as required by law.

    ☐ b. By removing the defendant(s) from the premises and putting the plaintiff in possession after giving notice of removal to the defendant(s) as required by law. The defendant's(s') property was taken to the warehouse listed below for storage.

    ☐ c. By giving notice of removal to the defendant(s) as required by law and by leaving the defendant's(s') property on the premises and locking the premises in accordance with the written request of the plaintiff which is attached.

☐ 2. I have failed to remove the defendant(s) from the premises for the following reason:

    ☐ a. The plaintiff requested that the Writ be returned because the defendant(s) satisfied the obligation to the plaintiff.

    ☐ b. The plaintiff failed to advance the expenses of removal and one month's storage after being asked to do so.

    ☐ c. Other: *(specify)*

Name And Address Of Warehouse

Fee Paid	Date Received	Signature Of Deputy Sheriff Making Return
$		
Fee Paid By	Date Executed	Name Of Deputy Sheriff (Type Or Print)
	Date Returned	County Of Sheriff

AOC-CV-401, Rev. 11/99
© 1999 Administrative Office of the Courts

SAMPLE

SAMPLE

COMMERCIAL LEASE AGREEMENT

Between

(Landlord) & (Tenant)

Date:_____

LOCATION AND DESCRIPTION OF PROPERTY:

BUSINESS NAME:

1. This **LEASE AGREEMENT** is for _____ months beginning on_____ and ending on_____.

2. This **COMMERICAL SPACE** is being leased to_____ for the purpose of:_____ AS IS, WHERE IS WITH NO IMPLIED WARRANTIES OR REPRESENTATIONS.

3. **BRIEF DESCRIPTION OF BUSINESS:**

4. The space is being leased for the business described. Any **ILLEGAL OR UNLAWFUL** activity will result in immediate eviction. Business will not create anyhardship or nuisance to surrounding tenants and be in compliance with all local and state ordinances and laws.

5. The lease payment is due on the **FIRST DAY** of each month.

6. The **LEASE PAYMENT** is: _____per month.

7. Payment will be considered **LATE** after the **5TH DAY** of the month. A late fee of $ 50.00 will be added to the lease payment if paid after the 5th day of the month.

8. A **DEPOSIT** of _____ will be paid. The deposit cannot be applied to any rent due. It will be used for repair/maintenance and clean-up. The tenant will be responsible for any repairs/damages that exceed the deposit. Space must be in original condition upon completion of the lease or damages will be collected.

9. The space utilized will be approximately _____ square feet.

10. All **UTILITIES** will be placed in the tenant's name prior to move-in. (electric, gas, water)

11. The tenant will **MAINTAIN THE EXTERIOR** exterior part of their building area. (no trash, debris or unsightly items will be around the exterior building area)

12. Any **IMPROVEMENTS,MODIFICATIONS, REMODELING** done to the leased space must be **APPROVED** by the landlord and submitted in writing.

13. The tenant will be responsible for all **REPAIRS AND MAINTENANCE EXCLUDING THE ROOF.**

14. **PARKING** is located as designated and agreed upon. _____parking spaces will be assigned. Any other parking must be approved by the landlord.

15. The tenant is responsible for **INSURANCE** that covers the interior and their belongings and possessions.

16. The tenant is responsible for any needed **LOCAL AND STATE PERMITS AND LICENSES.**

17. **NON-PAYMENT OF RENT** will result in **EVICTION**. The tenant will be responsible for court, attorney fees incurred for collection of the rent.

18. If the **TENANT TERMINATES** this agreement prior to the time listed, they will be responsible for the entire length of the lease..

19. If **FALSE INFORMATION** is submitted on this lease agreement, the landlord has the right to terminate this lease agreement.

20. The landlord is authorized with the tenant's permission to obtain a **CREDIT REPORT, BACKGROUND CHECK AND BUSINESS REFERENCES.**

I AGREE TO THESE TERMS AND CONDITONS SET FORTH:

Business Tenant: Landlord
Address: Address:
Telephone: Telephone:

SAMPLE

SAMPLE

TENANT SELECTION CRITERIA CHECKLIST

1. _____Arrived on time for appointment

2. _____Proper documentation available (driver's license, references, fees, deposit)

3. _____Application filled out completely.

4. _____Information is verifiable

5. _____Can pay full deposit and full month's rent

6. _____Verifiable income / employment

7. _____Employment is stable for_____months.

8. _____Income is at least three times the rent amount.

9. _____Financial obligations are no more than _____% of income.

10. _____Satisfactory credit history (bankruptcy?)

11. _____Credit references provided

12. _____Lived at current residence for _____months.

13. _____ Gave notice to present landlord.

14. _____No prior evictions

15. _____No problems with previous landlords and/or landlord can be contacted.

16. _____Deposit returned from previous landlord.

17. _____No complaints or police reports regarding disturbing the peace, nuisance, etc.

18. _____No pets or willing to sign a pet agreement. (type of pet)

Total of yes answers: _____

SAMPLE

LANDLORD'S NOTICE TO VACATE

Date:

Attention:

To the above tenant and all others residing and in possession of the below premises:

Address:

You are hereby requested to quit, vacate and deliver possession thereof to the undersigned on or before_____ 20_____.

This notice to vacate is due to your breach of tenancy:

Should you fail, refuse, neglect to pay your rent, cure the breach or vacate said premises within said_____days from this notice, I will take legal action as the law requires to evict you from the premises. You are fully responsible for all present and future rents due under your tenancy Agreement. You have therefore been advised that you will be evicted if you refuse to vacate.

Signed:_____

FLOW CHART FOR PURCHASING REAL ESTATE

RETURN ON INVESTMENT   **COST**   **LOCATION**

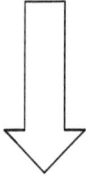

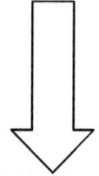

RETURN ON INVESTMENT IN TEN YEARS	KNOW YOUR COST COMPARE THE COSTS	STABLE AREA INCOME OF AREA
KEEP EXPENSES DOWN	CAN YOU DO REPAIRS? MAINTENANCE COST EXPENSES	WILL THE PROPERTY RETAIN ITS VALUE?
CHARGE THE RIGHT AMOUNT FOR RENT		WHAT IS THE DISTANCE TO THE PROPERTY?

PROPERTY OWNER'S FINANCIAL FLOW CHART

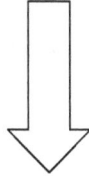

⬇

**YOU MUST KEEP UP TO 25% OF YOUR INCOME
FOR TIMES WHEN YOUR INVESTMENTS ARE VACANT.**

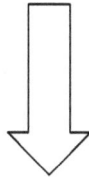

⬇

**YOU MUST KEEP RECORDS FOR THE I.R.S AND YOURSELF THAT INCLUDE ALL
YOUR EXPENSES INCLUDING REPAIRS AND MAINTENANCE.**

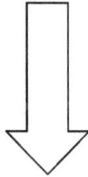

⬇

**YOU MUST HAVE AN ESCROW ACCOUNT FOR EMERGENCIES THAT COVERS
2-3 MONTHSOF RENTAL INCOME.**

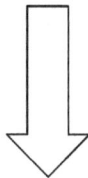

⬇

**YOU NEED A PLACE TO STORE SUPPLIES, MAINTENANCE ITEMS, APPLIANCES
AND ALL NECESSARY ITEMS FOR YOUR RENTALS.**

RENTAL FLOW CHART – 10 STEPS FROM PRE-SCREENING TO LEASE SIGNING

1. **Advertise & Pre-screen with newspaper ads, online**

2. **Schedule Showing**

3. **Prepare for the showing Application prepared**

4. **Show the property Ask questions Inspect things**

5. **Have prospective tenant fill out the application**

6. **Accept application with any fees and/or deposit**

7. **Verify and check application**

8. **Check credit and background**

9. **Review all information to make a decision on applicant.**

10. **Application approved or denied**

SAMPLE

REAL ESTATE ACQUISTION WORKSHEET

_____ Purchase Price of property

_____ Estimated price after fix-up

_____ Down Payment

_____ Closing Cost

_____ Appraisal

_____ Termite service

_____ Misc.

_____ **TOTAL EXPENSE TO PURCHASE**

_____ Budget to fix up

_____ **TOTAL FIX-UP COST**

_____ Payment for ____months

_____ Property Tax

_____ Insurance

_____ Cost of your capital

_____ Cost of your time

_____ **TOTAL HOLDING COST**

_____ Advertising costs

_____ Commission

_____ Sale closing cost

_____ **TOTAL SALES COST**

_____ **Sales price** (subtract the following)

_____ Mortgage payoffs

_____ Expense to buy

_____ Total fix up cost

_____ Total holding cost

_____ Total sales cost

_____ **YOUR PROFIT**

SAMPLE

RENT RECEIPT

Date: _____

Property Address: _____

Received from: _____the sum of $_____

Landlord: _____

Balance Due: $_____

Paid by: cash, check, money order
(circle one)

SAMPLE

TIME FOR REPAIRS

Date:

Tenant:

Property Address:

You have notified us of the following situation with your rental property:

_____

_____

_____

_____

We expect to respond to this situation by the following date:

_____

The situation may require the following:

_____

_____

_____

If there is a delay in responding to your situation, we will notify you as soon as possible.

We will contact you at:_____telephone_____telephone

SAMPLE

TENANT MINOR MAINTENANCE ITEMS

1. Tenant will fix leaky faucets that require minimum repair.

2. Tenant will check for water leaks. (under the sink, plumbing fixtures, exterior water faucets)

3. Tenant will fix running toilets that require minimum repair.

4. Tenant will inspect smoke detectors and carbon monoxide detectors and replace batteries as needed.

5. Tenant will be responsible for lawn maintenance if stated in the lease. (mowing, weed eating, trimming)

6. Tenant will notify the landlord with maintenance issues in a timely manner.

7. Tenant will use reasonable care to maintain the property in good condition.

SAMPLE

MOVE-OUT LETTER

Date:

Name of Tenant:

Address of Property:

Dear_____

In order for us to mutually end our landlord/tenant relationship in a positive way, this move-out letter will describe how we expect the property to be left as well as our procedure for returning security deposits.

The property should be left in the same condition it was in when you moved in. Normal wear and tear is expected. Attached is a copy of the move-in inspection list that you received before you signed your lease.

The following should be cleaned:

Floors

Vacuum carpet and rugs

Mop all tile or vinyl floors

Wipe walls, baseboards as needed

Wipe kitchen cabinets inside and outside, empty of all food

Clean kitchen sink and countertops

Clean refrigerator inside and outside, empty of all food. (leave running)

Clean stove, oven, microwave   (inside and outside)

Clean bathtubs, toilets, sinks and all plumbing fixtures.

Remove all trash

SAMPLE

Remove all items and belongings

Remove all items on the exterior of the property

Disconnect all utility services

Fill out a change of address form

Once the property is cleaned and everything is removed, call to arrange for the return of the keys.

You must give a forwarding address to mail your deposit.

Security deposits will be returned in person or at the forwarding address provided. Any items deducted from your security deposit will be listed in writing. Deposits will be returned within thirty days after move-out date.

SAMPLE

PROPERTY RULES AND REGULATIONS

1. **SANITATION AND GARBAGE**
   The tenant shall maintain the property rented to them clean and free of garbage and debris at all times. Garbage shall be disposed of in designated containers and picked up accordingly. No hazardous substances or materials to be disposed of in containers.

2. **CONDUCT IN PREMISES AND COMMON AREAS**
   a) All household items including furniture shall remain inside the property. No junk type items shall be outside the property.
   b) Tenant will not engage or create loud noise, sound or activity that disturbs other tenants. This includes loud talking, yelling or using profanity.
   c) Tenant shall not play any musical instrument, radio, music system, television so loud that it disturbs other residents.

USE OF THE PROPERTY AND COMMON AREAS
   a) Tenant is responsible for keeping their rental property secure.
   b) Tenant shall notify landlord if any door or window becomes broken or not useable.
   c) Tenant shall not use barbecues, grills or other outdoor cooking equipment indoors or use above another rental property.
   d) No bicycles, play equipment or outdoor toys shall be left in the common areas.
   e) Tenant shall not paint, wallpaper, alter property, change or install different locks or any other modification to the property without obtaining the landlord's permission in writing.
   f) Window coverings are restricted to blinds or window coverings. No other items may be hung in the windows.
   g) Damages to the appliances caused by negligence of the tenant shall be charged to the tenant.
   h) Tenants with pets are responsible to follow all state and local laws and ordinances. Pets must be on a lease while walking. Pet owners must clean-up waste from their pets. Pets left outside must be on a lease or in a fenced in area.

SAMPLE

Parking and Vehicles

a) No parking anywhere other than designated areas. No parking on the lawnor yard. Tenants may not use other tenant's parking spaces without permission.
b) No vehicles allowed that are unregistered or disabled. These vehicles will be towed.
c) No car washing, oil changing or car repairs to be conducted in the parking spaces.

All by-laws and covenants issued by the property/community must be abided by and followed by the tenant.

Tenant's signature:_____Date:_____

Landlord's signature:_____Date:_____

SAMPLE

AMENDMENT TO THE LEASE AGREEMENT

Date:

Tenant:_____

Property Address:_____

Date of Lease:_____

The tenant has agreed to the following changes and or additions to the lease agreement:

1._____

_____

_____

2._____

_____

_____

_____

_____

_____

Landlord:_____ Tenant:_____

APPENDIX II:
SOCIAL SECURITY REFERENCE NUMBERS

Verification that tenant is providing a legitimate social security number

Social Security number prefixes by state:

1.	Alabama	416-424
2.	Alaska	574
3.	Arizona	526-527
4.	Arkansas	429-432
5.	California	545-573
6.	Colorado	521-524
7.	Connecticut	040-049
8.	Delaware	221-222
9.	Florida	261-267
10.	Georgia	252-260
11.	Hawaii	575-576
12.	Idaho	518-519
13.	Illinois	318-361
14.	Indiana	303-317
15.	Iowa	478-485
16.	Kansas	509-515
17.	Kentucky	400-407
18.	Louisiana	433-439
19.	Maine	004-007
20.	Maryland	212-220
21.	Massachusetts	010-034

22.	Michigan	362-386
23.	Minnesota	468-477
24.	Missouri	486-500
25.	Mississippi	425-428
26.	Montana	516-517
27.	New Hampshire	001-003
28.	North Carolina	237-246
29.	Nebraska	505-508
30.	North Dakota	501-502
31.	New Mexico	525
32.	New York	050-134
33.	New Jersey	135-158
34.	Nevada	530
35.	Ohio	268-302
36.	Oklahoma	440-448
37.	Oregon	540-544
38.	Pennsylvania	159-211
39.	Rhode Island	035-039
40.	South Carolina	247-251
41.	South Dakota	503-504
42.	Texas	449-467
43.	Tennessee	408-415
44.	Utah	528-529
45.	Vermont	008-009
46.	Virginia	223-231
47.	West Virginia	232-236
48.	Wyoming	520
49.	Washington	531-539
50.	Wisconsin	387-399

APPENDIX III:
WEBSITE RESOURCES FOR LANDLORDS

landlord.com
(information for landlords)

landlordstatelaws.com
(state laws for landlords and tenants)

landlordassociation.org
(state laws for landlords and tenants)

totalrealestatesolutions.com
(free real estate forms)

mrlandlord.com
(information for landlords)